# Timeless Leadership Principles
## Building Champions for Life

Jim Kunau & Kent Schlichtemeier

Champions for Life Publishing—Irvine, CA
ISBN: 978-0-578-94515-6
Library of Congress Control Number: 2021913213
Title: *Timeless Leadership Principles: Building Champions For Life*
Author: Jim Kunau & Kent Schlichtemeier
Digital distribution | 2021
Paperback | 2021

Published in the United States by New Book Authors Publishing

# Timeless Leadership Principles

## Building Champions for Life

# Table of Contents

# Preface

Kick-off was scheduled for 7:00 p.m. Jim felt a calm confidence about how his Orange Lutheran Lancers would perform in the game even though they were playing the 5th ranked team in the pre-season poll for California. Mighty Mater Dei, the perennial power and best-known high school football program in Southern California, made for an exhilarating season opener for the team, school, and fans. Nine thousand partisans filled the Santa Ana Bowl, split evenly between the competitors, curious to see if the Lancer's showing last year against the Mater Dei Monarchs was a fluke. The Lancers had lost to Coach Bruce Rollinson's squad, 21-20, when they failed on a two-point conversion on the last play of the game. Mater Dei's players, who understandably thought they would demolish the upstart Lancers last year, seemed more focused for tonight's battle in their warm-ups. And even though Orange Lutheran was the home team, the contest was being played in the Monarch's stadium, since it could hold the anticipated 8,000-10,000 fans while the Lancer's regular home stadium was crammed at 4,500. Jim's team was poised and confident after eight months of diligent training.

Jim had no doubt that his squad was ready for the 7:00 p.m. kickoff. As their pregame preparations continued to unfold his only unease was centered on 6:30 p.m. when he had invited the fathers, stepfathers, uncles, and grandfathers of the 75 players to meet him in the spacious locker room.

There is something special about locker rooms before significant football games. Emotions are heightened, and the sense of sweeping urgency begins to swell. Emotions uncork and begin to boil within each athlete like great thoroughbreds suddenly confined to the cramped quarters of the starting gate. Jim left his team's field preparations at 6:28 p.m. and walked into the locker room at exactly 6:30 p.m., where he would have 15 minutes alone with the most important men in his players' lives. The men were both curious and quiet, and instinctively intent.

He had them form a ring around him with their backs to the lockers and explained why they had been invited. First, they gathered to hear a story about life's priorities and second, to share a uniquely special time with their sons and grandsons. Finally, just by their mere presence, they were there to inspire these special, courageous young men.

Before he began his illustration, Jim shared with them that it was an honor to have them in the locker room. He told them that pregame locker room atmospheres take on an almost sacred aura, not because the world is going to hang on the outcome of a high school football game, but because it is a time when the depths of players' and coaches' emotions and spirits reach out and connect with one another in a raw, open way. Locker rooms have an unusual knack for stripping away artificial barriers that tend to segregate people, such as status, income, and ancestry.

In the middle of the locker room was a table with a large empty glass pitcher sitting on it. A few months earlier Jim had read a wonderful story which he would now share with the men to highlight their importance as leaders. From below the table he pulled out two pieces of wood and placed them inside the pitcher filling most of its space. Jim asked rhetorically, "Is it full?" After a short pause, Jim then reached for a couple of cups of gravel and dumped them into the space around the wood. He again asked, "Is it full?" No one spoke to break the solemn silence created by the unique atmosphere. Next he poured in sand to fill in the remaining crevices. "Well, now is it full?" again peering around, locking eyes with many. Finally, he pulled out a water bottle and poured it in until it filled the pitcher completely. Now it was full. He hesitated a moment before asking one final rhetorical question: "Do you know what the lesson is?" Still there was only respectful silence. "If you don't take care of the big things first in your life, you will end up not having any room for them. And what are the big things? They are the relationships we form with the Lord, our families, our friends, our co-workers. This is the truth that I want you to remember most about tonight for the sake of your sons and grandsons." He went on to instruct them that when their sons, nephews, and grandsons walked in the locker room in a couple of minutes they were to immediately find and embrace each one, telling them they loved them. This was shared not as a mild-mannered request, but as something that was a clear expectation that was part of the privilege for being there. For the players we knew who had no one there for them from their families, a coach was assigned to be their surrogate father.

A few moments later the players began filing in, each being greeted by emotional hugs from the men they most admired in life. Sadly for some, the embrace was like a long lost reunion breaking the icy bonds of time and distance created by divorce, detachment, or dysfunction. After a few minutes Jim began speaking, turning his attention to the red-clad cloud of determined teenagers surrounding him, who were flanked by their own fathers, uncles, and grandfathers. He reminded them of the great love that radiated among them and challenged them to passionately play tonight's game out of their love of God, family, school, and one another. Finally, Jim shared Hebrews 12:1:

*"Therefore, since we are surrounded by such a great cloud of witnesses, let us throw off everything that hinders and the sin that so easily entangles, and let us run with perseverance the race marked out for us."*

That memorable night in the locker room a group of boys was surrounded by men who loved them and in turn inspired them to compete boldly in a game of football. Each day of our lives we are empowered to run the race of life with similar conviction witnessed in the heroes and martyrs of the past who surround us, urging us to make a significant impact with our lives.

Good locker room speeches have a debatable impact on the actual outcome of a game. But they can be a special vehicle for creating indelible memories and feelings, and even more, they serve to motivationally remind young warriors about the truth and what is most important in life; that is, what is worth struggling for, living for, and sacrificing for.

As Christians, we strive to develop a character that embodies the "truth" in life as modeled by Jesus who proclaimed: "I am the Way, the Truth, and the Life" (John 14:6). The template for "truth" in our world today can be found in the life of Jesus who declares: "I am the light of the world. Whoever follows me will never walk in darkness, but will have the light of life" (John 8:12). This pursuit of "truth" and "light" were the pillars of the 'Mission" of the Lancer football program to *Build Champions for Life.*

Truth is light, and light illuminates the darkness. Without it we stumble in darkness, unsure of our footing, not knowing when we will inevitably step into the next pothole of life. The power of the light of truth should never be underestimated nor should our fidelity to it ever waver. The path of truth is not easy, but it is the only path that yields a life of honor where trustworthy and lasting relationships are possible.

Nations and empires have fallen because they abandoned truth for expediency in service of their own desires and goals as they fully embraced the fruits of "the ends justify the means" mantra. In the midst of the Great COVID Pandemic, malevolent incivility, and the acrimonious 2020 presidential election, truth has become an elusive commodity in our culture. But truth is also something more. The bible describes Jesus as the embodiment of grace and truth, and that if we know Him who is absolute truth, then that truth will set us free.

The pages of this book are a compilation of insights gained by two individuals who have devoted a combined 75 years of service as leaders in education and athletics and have observed the difference that following the "truths" of Christ – the "light" of the world can make in one's life. This book is about much more than becoming "champions" in the athletic arena or business board room, but rather about becoming *Champions for Life* committed to affecting lasting, positive change in the lives of many. True *Champions* are exemplary leaders forged with strong character who courageously pursue noble causes to help fill the "pitcher of life" with the big things that affect others in significant ways. *Champions for Life,* just like "champions" in athletics, eschew lives of comfort and ease to create change for the better in individuals and cultures throughout the world.

# Introduction

In October of 2006, on one of the most thrilling days of our lives, we spent an afternoon with the greatest living coach in America: John Wooden. We felt like Greek adolescents sitting at the feet of Aristotle, questioning the master teacher about everything from championship team excellence to human relations. At one point, Kent mentioned to Coach Wooden that he had read that he always kept a small cross in his pocket during his coaching career. Whenever he felt angry or agitated, instead of losing his composure, he would reach into his pocket to feel the cross as a reminder that there were more critical things in life than winning basketball games. While Kent was recollecting this for him, Coach Wooden wryly smiled and reached into his pocket as we sat in his favorite restaurant in Encino, pulling out that very cross before placing it on the table for us to observe. It was evident this wasn't just some lucky charm or an interesting anecdote for his books or conversations, but that he leaned on his faith throughout his entire 99 years on this earth. When we think about the embodiment of a *Champion for Life*, Coach Wooden, a paragon of epic proportions comes to mind. He epitomizes all the core qualities of what it means to be an exemplary leader and human being.

People like John Wooden, Mother Teresa, and Martin Luther King Jr. demonstrated that it is possible to live a life of great virtue and purpose. What was it that made these leaders such *Champions*? At the core of their beings, integrity ruled. Their actions were in complete alignment with their words and commitments. Because they displayed such a high degree of integrity, the trust and respect of others naturally flowed. In virtually every study conducted where people are asked to identify the most important quality they seek in leaders, integrity is inevitably the most valued virtue and the foundation for honorable character. Integrity comes from the Latin "integritas" which means "wholeness, completeness, and entirety." *Champions for Life* seamlessly epitomize harmony of word and deed. The congruity of their actions and values define integrity and cannot help but elicit admiration and trust.

Just as important, *Champions for Life* cultivate peace of mind and purpose which is reflected in a serene confidence allowing them to navigate the most treacherous waters while effectively modeling for others. This is because, for them, success is measured not by wins or losses, but rather by the secure knowledge they have, in the words of Coach Wooden, "done their best to become the best they are capable of becoming" while never betraying their core principles.

*Champions for Life* have come to terms with what it means to pursue and experience *real* success. There are fundamentally two divergent perspectives on success. The first is society's, which claims that the scoreboard, the accumulation of material goods, or the attainment of fame and power, are the measures of success. There are, however, several problems with this hierarchical perspective where a few succeed and most fail. The reality is when our mindset is acquisitive and temporal in nature we can never win or accumulate enough to satisfy ourselves or our constituents. Consequently, we are inevitably left with a haunting emptiness, like the desperately thirsty lost in a vast desert.

There is an alternative way to view success. From a process perspective, we define it as "unselfishly giving your best every day regardless of circumstances." "Unselfishly" connotes other-centeredness that frees us from the chains and limitations of self-absorption. It fosters an attitude of genuine concern for others that yields respect from superiors and peers as well as admiration from followers. "Giving your best every day" is the inspirational and contagious commitment to summon and release every fiber of your being in relentless pursuit of a worthy cause. "Every day" presumes consistency; that is, maximum effort and a deep caring for others are a natural part of who you are - someone who can always be counted on. The Latin imperative *Machte Virtute* can be found inscribed in various team meeting rooms, which is the command to increase in excellence in all you do and to conquer through character. It is measured in comparison to our best selves, not in relation to others. There is an old saying which captures this concept: *"There is nothing noble in being superior to someone else, the only true nobility in life comes from being superior to your former self."* Coach Wooden shared with us that one of the greatest lessons his father taught him was never to compare himself to anyone else, that the only thing that mattered was striving to be the best he could be. Hence, Coach Wooden defined success as, "Peace of mind which is the direct result of self-satisfaction in knowing you made the effort to become the best you are capable of becoming." Finally, "regardless of circumstances" reminds us that doing the right thing with focus and determination is easy when there are no challenging circumstances. That environment requires very little character. It is only when circumstances are compellingly difficult that worthy character is built and revealed.

Legendary De La Salle High School Football Coach Bob Ladoceur, who coached his teams to an unparalleled 160 game winning streak was widely recognized as one of the nation's most successful coaches at any level in any sport. In the midst of the streak he explained: "Kids will fight for you if you stand for more than winning… It boils down to what you believe as a person, how life should be lived, how people should be treated … We don't look at the scoreboard. It's about commitment and effort… If it was about wins and losses, we would have lost a long time ago." Those who sustain success like Coach Ladoceur over a lengthy period of time almost always have a deeper purpose or cause which impels them to sacrifice and find ways to constantly improve without ever lowering their commitment.

Success should be defined in larger terms than our own personal gains and accomplishments. Worldly success often aims too low by focusing on *taking* from life. Significance, on the other hand, is what we *give* to life, how we deliberately focus on adding value to the lives of others. In the book *Season of Life*, Coach Joe Ehrmann of Gilman High School from Baltimore, states that one of the greatest disservices being done to young men today is that they are given a harmful threefold criteria for what it means to be a man. He identifies these components of "false masculinity" as athletic ability, sexual conquest, and economic success. He challenges us to define true manhood instead as the ability to establish and grow meaningful relationships through developing the capacity to love and be loved. He insightfully shares that the second criterion for healthy masculinity ought to be to embrace a purpose that is bigger than our own individual dreams, wants, and desires. At the end of our lives, we ought to be able to trust that the world became a better place because we lived and loved, and were other-centered and other-focused.

The reality is that worldly "success" is available to few, but excellence as in the *Machte Virtute* sense, is available for all. When success is defined and recognized in a way that each person on a team, organization, or family has a meaningful chance of achieving, by "unselfishly giving your best every day," you have created the opportunity to have a positive impact on everyone. For example, one of the greatest players the Orange Lutheran football program produced over Jim's 19 years at the helm was a young man by the name of Vishal. His parents emigrated from India and understandably had no interest in football. Vishal, however, learned to love football early on and was drawn to the gridiron. By his senior year the 5'11", 175 pound linebacker was a tough, competitive football player. Both on and off the field Vishal was the proverbial rising tide that lifted all boats. His passion and unselfishness were contagious. He made everyone around him a better player and person by constantly and enthusiastically modeling what it meant to unselfishly give your best every day, devoting himself to a larger purpose. He was a unanimous selection as a team captain and yet the highest he ever rose on the depth chart was to third string. He played in only a couple of games his senior year when his team led by substantial margins. By the world's standards, Vishal was a failure as he only cheered from the sidelines for those who made headlines in the newspapers. However, he was constantly honored and held up as a template of excellence because of his commitment to maximize his talents and those of his teammates. It was no surprise to anyone that he went on to become ASB Vice-President at Cal Berkeley and now works for a prestigious firm in the San Francisco Bay area.

*Champions for Life* are powerful difference makers in their families, teams, organizations, communities, and country. Champions may outwardly be ordinary people, but they are extraordinary leaders with an unwavering commitment to integrity and humble service to help enable others reach heights they cannot take themselves. In the pages of this book you will be introduced to twelve timeless principles that help you become a *Champion for Life.*

# Chapter 1
## "Champions Face God First"

*"Never be afraid to trust an unknown future to a known God."*
(Corrie ten Boom)

"On your mark, get set, GO!" These familiar words are first heard in life at a very young age when adults encourage youngsters to race in fun competitions. The thrill of hurtling toward the finish line brings big smiles to children eager to win recognition and receive affectionate affirmation. There is something inherently exhilarating about moving fast whether running, driving a car, piloting a boat, or even flying an airplane. This urgent pace, however, seems to pitilessly govern most of our existence as we race through each day, with hours seeming to be shorter and shorter with every technological advancement. Studies show that this frenetic pace of life leaves us feeling frazzled as we run from one thing to the next, like proverbial caged hamsters. For most adults waking each morning, the alarm clock has become the substitute starter crying out, 'On your mark...!'

As we GO, GO, GO when our feet first hit the floor in the mornings we often find ourselves rushing to check cell phones for recent emails or text messages, ESPN for updated scores, or CNBC for stock prices. Life in the 21$^{st}$ century is a bombardment of information combined with fast paced activities focused on consumption, participation, and acquisition. Sadly, there are deleterious costs to frenzied lives. Anxiety disorders, insomnia, hypertension, and ulcers are common maladies on the rise. Both "quality" and "quantity" of time spent with loved ones necessary to foster meaningful relationships has shrunk dramatically. In 1900, the majority of families spent an average of seven hours a day of interactive time together. Fast forward to the 21$^{st}$ century, and that key barometer of family closeness and viability has drastically declined to a paltry seven minutes a day. Being busy is also the prime reason Americans often fail to vote, attend church, or read their Bibles. Having lost our sense of balance, we begin to feel overwhelmed and miserable, unable to free ourselves from the never ending onslaught of seemingly inescapable duties and routines.

The depressing feeling of being a powerless prisoner to the daily drudgery often arises from striving to meet each day's demands strictly on our own abilities. We are taught from a young age to become self-sufficient as quickly as possible. While independence certainly has its advantages, taken to an extreme it leads to isolation and a corresponding exaggeration of capabilities. This tends to produce the mindset that we are perfectly capable of navigating through life on our accord. Fortunately, there are innumerable "thumb prints" from God providing evidence in the natural world that our existence is not random, haphazard, or isolated. Consider the protective ability of the bombardier beetle to mix two chemicals in its body to create a gas at 212 degrees farenheit (the boiling point) to stun predators so that it can scurry to safety. Or look at the human eye and how the pupil can dilate and constrict automatically thousands of times each day to protect sensitive retina cells and to filter just enough light to be able to see. Or consider the perfect distance between the earth and sun preventing us from burning up or freezing to death and, in fact, making life possible. The miracles observed in nature exclaim the fundamental truth of life: There MUST be a God! In Genesis 1:1 we read, "In the beginning God created the heavens and the earth." This simple, all important, declaration changes everything. If you believe that statement, you can believe every word that follows in the Bible which reveals that God so loved us that He saved us and is *eager to help us daily.*

The reality is that everyone lives by faith. For devout Christians, it takes faith to believe there is a God who created our world and us. After all, where did God come from? Even the most diehard atheist faces a similar dilemma with what philosophers call the argument of the first cause; that is, where did the random elements come from that produced our planet and our lives? Did they just exist without cause? Both perspectives, the believer's and the atheist's, (and everyone in between for that matter), are reliant on faith. It is a little like the joke about the difference between "Dog Theology" and "Cat Theology." The dog looks at the person who feeds it and cares for it, and says: "You must be God." The cat looks at a similar person and says "Since you feed me and take care of me, I must be God." Like the cat, many people have a "faith" that sees themselves as the center of the universe and the sole author of their destiny, unknowingly unplugging themselves from the greater reality. The good news is that there is a God, and we are not Him. The *Champion for Life* humbly understands that displacing God is folly and instead finds God to be the source of wisdom, peace, joy, and happiness.

Laura Hillenbrand, in her New York Times best-selling book titled *Unbroken,* chronicled the extraordinary life of Louis Zamperini and the harrowing ordeals he experienced during World War II. One of the greatest distance runners of any era, Louis competed as an 18- year-old in the 1936 Berlin Summer Olympics. Had the war not interrupted his career it is likely Zamperini would have become the first athlete to shatter the 4-minute mile barrier. Sadly, the war in the Pacific did much more than detour an astonishing track competitor; it set him on a path of suffering few men have ever survived.

Flying as a crewman in a B-24, nicknamed the "Green Hornet" on May 27, 1943, Louis barely survived the plane's plunge into the middle of the Pacific after experiencing catastrophic engine failure. For the next 47 days, on a small life raft with two other officers, Zamperini would barely survive thirst, starvation, sharks, and even a Japanese fighter pilot's strafing. Unfortunately, the island he ultimately washed up on was occupied by the Japanese, marking not an end to his ordeal, but the beginning of a tortuous 26-month exile in brutal POW camps.

In August, 1945, Louis returned to America a shell of the vigorous athlete he had been a few short years earlier. He had been starved, repeatedly beaten, and subjected to incessant psychological trauma. Zamperini's post war life dissolved into alcoholism and abuse as he was haunted by everything that had happened to him and chased by the demonic memories of a particularly savage prison guard known as "The Bird."

It was only when Louis agreed to attend a Billy Graham Crusade with his wife, Cynthia, that he was finally freed from his personal demons. On a starlit night in Los Angeles in 1949, Louis listened intently as Graham spoke of how even in the midst of man's most awful suffering, He gives us the grace to go forward. "What God asks of man," said Graham, "is faith. His invisibility is the truest test of faith. To know who sees him, God makes Himself unseen." Louis went back in his mind to the 47 days on the raft boiling in the sun amidst the circling sharks while dying of thirst. He recalled a promise he had made to the Lord in the midst of that excruciating situation, "If you will save me, I will serve you forever." When Billy Graham invited those who wanted to give their hearts to the Lord to come forward, Louis strode up to the makeshift altar and surrendered his life to a loving Savior. From that night forward, the nightmares stopped, and the alcoholism ended. Whereas independence from God had brought him to his knees, his newfound dependence on the saving grace of God removed the shackles and burdens that were shattering and crushing his life. Grace is God's riches given to us freely at Christ's expense. As Jesus promises in John 8:32: "You shall know the truth and the truth shall set you free." Zamperini's faith in Christ set him free that night, and he entered a faith-filled freedom he enjoyed until his passing in 2014.

Despite the harried nature of our lives, we would be wise to proactively set time aside to spend with God. To 'fly solo' means missing out on essential, priceless benefits that can only be derived from the Author of joy and salvation. There is a valuable antidote to "going it alone" that we can glean from the life of Moses, the biblical hero who led the Israelites out of bondage in Egypt. Moses was an ordinary shepherd diligently engaged in caring for his flock, when his simple life was unexpectedly interrupted, as described in Exodus 3:1-4:

> Now Moses was tending the flock of Jethro his father-in-law, the priest of Midian. And he led the flock to the back of the desert, and came to Horeb, the mountain of God. And the Angel of the Lord appeared to him in a flame of fire from the midst of a bush. So he looked and behold, the bush was burning with fire, but the bush was not consumed. Then Moses said, "I will now turn aside and see this great sight why the bush does not burn." So when the Lord saw that he turned aside to look, God called to him from the midst of the bush and said, "Moses, Moses!" And he said, "Here I am."

Moses, like us, was busy with life. Thankfully for the generations of chained Hebrew laborers waiting to be freed from Pharaoh's tyranny, he stepped off the treadmill of life long enough to *turn to the burning bush where God was* preparing to empower his life and change the course of history. It is interesting to note that the Bible records when the Lord saw that Moses looked to Him, He spoke. We can only speculate how the destiny of the Hebrew slaves would have dramatically differed had Moses not looked to God. Moses PAUSED to spend time with God, enabling him to discover his calling to lead others and shape the course of history. The course of his life shifted from one governed by himself or chosen for him by others, to one directed by the Creator of the Universe. God is still eager to pave the paths of ordinary people like us today to serve Him as leaders.

There is, of course, much to do in our lives. Working hard, maximizing our talents, and utilizing our time effectively are hallmarks of people committed to excellence. However, there is an empowerment that comes from first communicating with God on a regular basis. We can learn a great deal from Mother Teresa, who used her given days to the fullest as she tended to the needs of thousands of people with compassion and love. Yet despite the endless needs and challenges and demands that faced her every day, Mother Teresa reported that she regularly began each day of her work by spending a full two hours in prayer. Her faith was strengthened by growing closer to God through prayer, teaching us that the stronger our connection with the Lord, the greater our capacity to love. She demonstrated that the more we love, the greater our desire will be to serve and make a difference. But the source of her love and devotion was not herself. Prayer, simply put, was the wellspring of her strength, inspiration, and love. Minus daily communication with the Lord she felt incapable, in her words, of being, "a little pencil in the hand of God who is writing his love letter to the world in this way, through works of love." Mother Teresa discovered purpose and power to minister to the orphans, the sick, and dying after intentionally facing God first. She embodied the principle that we should strive to live life in such a way that those who know you, but don't know God, will come to know God because they know you. Throughout her life, Mother Teresa, even in the midst of the most dire circumstances, understood and embraced the God who nourished her soul as well as the hearts and souls of the greatest outcasts to whom she devoted her life and energy.

When we don't take the time to commune with God on a regular basis, our lives and destinies are lamentably and inevitably altered. The good news is, God desires to spend time with us. God speaks to people today through prayer and the reading of His word. He is the beacon for our lives. Sometimes He is the light emanating from a burning bush, calling us to action, or sometimes, as in the following story, He is the light shielding us from certain calamity:

Canadian Coast Guard Petty Officer: Please divert your course 15 degrees to the South to avoid disaster.

American Sea Captain: Recommend you divert your course 15 degrees to the North to avoid a collision.

Canadian: Negative. You must divert your course 15 degrees to the South to avoid a collision.

American: This is the Captain of a US Navy ship. I say again, divert YOUR course.

Canadian: No, I say again, you must divert YOUR course.

American: This is the Aircraft Carrier USS Lincoln, the second largest ship in the United States' Atlantic Fleet. We are accompanied by three destroyers, three cruisers, and numerous support vessels. I demand that you change your course 15 degrees north – I say again, that's one five degrees north – or counter-measure will be undertaken to ensure the safety of this ship.
Canadian: Sir, this is a lighthouse. It's your call.

Christian sage and author C.S. Lewis reminds us that there are two kinds of people: "Those who say to God, 'Thy will be done' and those to whom God says, [as the Canadian Officer above essentially says], 'Thy will be done.'" It's our call. As we reflect, we should remember that God is always present with His perpetual light to prevent us from crashing on the rocky coastline of any darkness we may experience in life. We are often like the imperious aircraft carrier captain with our egos preventing us from recognizing our need to seek and heed His wisdom and will for our lives. But fortunately, He is a constant, like a lighthouse or the North Star, there to protect and guide.

When time is not spent with God, a chasm will naturally develop. This void makes facing adversity in life a much more daunting and frightening proposition. Often when encountering difficulties we have a tendency to question what we perceive to be God's indifference and seeming unresponsiveness to our dilemmas. C.S. Lewis in *A Grief Observed* captured this age-old tension in the following words:

Meanwhile, where is God? This is one of the most disquieting symptoms. When you are happy, so happy that you have no sense of needing Him.... you will be – or so it feels – be welcomed with open arms. But go to Him when your need is desperate all other help is vain, and what do you find? A door slammed in your face, and a sound of bolting and double bolting on the inside. After that, silence.

This seeming absence of God is an illusion that is vividly dispelled in the following poem:

> One night I dreamed I was walking along the beach with the Lord. Many scenes from my life flashed across the sky.
>
> In each scene, I noticed footprints in the sand. Sometimes there were two sets of footprints, other times there was one only.
>
> This bothered me because I noticed that during the low periods of my life, when I was suffering from anguish, sorrow or defeat, I could see only one set of footprints, so I said to the Lord,
>
> "You promised me Lord, that if I followed you, you would walk with me always. But I have noticed that during the most trying periods of my life there has only been one set of footprints in the sand. Why, when I needed you most, have you not been there for me?"
>
> The Lord replied, "The years when you have seen only one set of footprints, my child, is when I carried you."

The single set of footprints left by the Lord carrying us in the face of challenges prompts us to ask not whether the Lord is behaving according to our expectations, but rather are we demonstrating, through our thoughts and deeds, that we are committed to being on His side? Are we committed to discovering, embracing, and enacting His will or do we treat him like a Ouija board trying to convince ourselves that our desires are "His will?" Some years ago prior to Orange Lutheran's kickoff against their chief rival Mater Dei, a television reporter asked Jim privately if he, as a Christian coach, believed that God was on their side. Without hesitating, he responded with an emphatic "Yes." Pausing as the reporter's eyes grew large with shock that he would make such an audacious claim, Jim went on to explain that he knew for a fact that God was on the side of every Orange Lutheran player, coach, and fan. And then Jim smiled and shared that he also knew for a fact that the Lord was on the side of every Mater Dei player, coach and fan. Jim said he knew this because 2,000 years ago Jesus sacrificed Himself for every single one of us so that we would not suffer the consequences of our sins. He closed the conversation by noting that therefore the question is never whether God is on our side, but rather whether we will choose to be on His?

Spending time with God is a source of wisdom. Unfortunately, many people today are obsessed with the lives, eccentricities, and antics of celebrities, hanging onto gossip headlines and every celebrity utterance. The media seemingly cannot release information fast enough to satisfy ravenous minds. Sadly, the superficial events of the day pique our interest and consume our curiosity. All of this focus on fleeting events and personalities, combined with neglecting the purposeful pursuit of wisdom, is producing a shallow society. Few today have the broad and deep perspective of life as did Solomon. Solomon was granted a rare privilege by God to "Ask for whatever you [Solomon] want me [God] to give you." Solomon did not ask for riches, a harem, or fame, instead replying to the Lord: "Give your servant a discerning heart…" (I Kings 3:5-9). God was so moved by Solomon's request that He not only granted him wisdom; but a kingdom and honors befitting the wisest person on earth. Solomon's example provides a simple, but powerful blueprint for living: first seek God and humbly ask for wisdom.

Spending time with God is a source of peace. Joseph Scriven in 1855, following the tragic deaths of not one but two fiancées, captured the importance of facing God first as he penned the words of the following timeless hymn:

What a Friend we have in Jesus, all our sins and griefs to bear!
What a privilege to carry everything to God in prayer!
O what peace we often forfeit, O what needless pain we bear,
All because we do not carry everything to God in prayer.
Have we trials and temptations? Is there trouble anywhere?
We should never be discouraged; take it to the Lord in prayer.
Can we find a friend so faithful who will all our sorrows share?

Jesus knows our every weakness; take it to the Lord in prayer.
Are we weak and heavy laden, cumbered with a load of care?
Precious Savior, still our refuge, take it to the Lord in prayer.
Do your friends despise, forsake you? Take it to the Lord in
prayer!

In His arms He'll take and shield you; you will find a solace
there.

It is essential to begin each day intentionally by carving out time for
our Creator – facing God first - and as the hymn writer encourages:
"Take it to the Lord in prayer… O what pain we often bear… O
what peace we often forfeit" all because we race, race, race without
faithfully spending time with the Author of Time.

Because we are not meant to live our lives in isolation, we also
need to encourage one another to seek refuge in the Lord. The story
is told in Africa of several villagers who converted to Christianity.
They would gather together for prayer each day in a nearby thicket.
Over time, each wore down a grassy path that led from his home to
the prayer gathering spot. If a believer would begin to neglect the
prayer time, another believer would kindly remark: "Brother, the
grass is beginning to grow in your path." Almost everyone leads
frantically busy lives and it is easy to disregard our relationship with
God, allowing the urgent to displace the paramount. Yet the paradox
is, the more we diligently cultivate our relationship with the Lord the
more effective we become in our most important responsibilities and
obligations. We also maintain a healthier disposition and more
balanced perspective on life's priorities.

Faith is believing in something greater than ourselves that gives us
purpose, hope, and a reason for living. It is, in the words of St. Paul,
"being sure of what we hope for and certain of what we do not see"
(Hebrews 11:1). We have to decide whether we are here to serve and
honor ourselves or to serve and honor God. It is critical that this
decision be a conscious one - not one dictated to us by others, or by
circumstance. And it is a decision that is made not once – but daily,
in our actual actions and personal disciplines. When we take time to
face God through our prayers or the reading of His word, we are
growing spiritually and honoring God Himself. The benefits of
honoring God are powerfully significant: "For the eyes of the Lord

range throughout the earth to strengthen those whose hearts are fully committed to Him" (II Chronicles 16:9). Too often, unless we see visible proof of His power, we doubt the unseen. After all, there is an old saying that some things have to be seen to be believed. But the inverse is also true: Some things have to be believed to be seen. The reward of faith, St. Augustine reminds us, is to "one day see what we believe."

There will come a time when we will literally stand face to face with God. It is mind boggling to begin to contemplate what we stand to inherit; to be with the saints who have gone on before us from our own families, as well as saints from throughout the ages. To be in the presence of the Almighty, the Prince of Peace, who has made it possible for us to be reunited with loved ones for eternity, is a powerful truth we should never let go of. That is the truth that should give us hope for today and courage for tomorrow. Doesn't it make sense to begin facing God now on a daily basis through His Word and prayer? The meaning of life, our true purpose, is too often blurred in today's sensory overloaded society. But gaining clarity by facing God first, by making Him THE priority, all things become possible in this fast-paced race of life. Wise men of yesterday sought the Lord in the manger. Wise men today continue to seek Him.

# "Champions Face God First"
*Championship Points*

*"But seek first his kingdom and his righteousness, and all these things will be given to you as well."*

(Matthew 6:33)

1. People tend to hurry through life solo, not recognizing there is a God who can help us.

2. Facing God FIRST gives strength for today and hope for tomorrow.

3. Faith based leaders look to God, not others, to determine their worth.

4. It is important to face God first in life for the following reasons:
   a. Gain clarity of purpose in life.
   b. Gain perspective on danger, fortifying us before the storms of life hit.
   c. Gain wisdom.
   d. Gain solace and peace.
   e. Remind us that we are not alone in life.

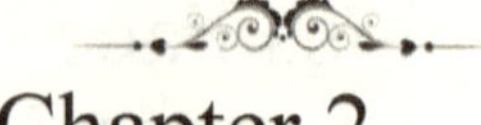

# Chapter 2
## "Champions Forge Strong Character"

*"Waste no more time arguing what a good man should be, be one."*
(Marcus Aurelius)

In 1991, billionaire investment guru Warren Buffet found himself in a very unusual situation. After the sudden resignation of the CEO of the Wall Street investment titan, Salomon Brothers, he was asked to select a replacement. Compounding the dilemma was a grave concern that if a new CEO was not identified quickly, Salomon clients and investors would likely abandon the firm. Mr. Buffet was given 48 hours to make this critical choice. With such a tight time parameter, he interviewed 12 executives already working at high levels within Salomon. Here is his recollection of the experience:

> I interviewed people regularly over a three or four-hour period. I didn't ask if they went to business school or for their resumes… I simply picked out who I felt was the best human being… He didn't have to throw a football 60 yards... But he had to bring qualities like honesty, steadfastness, humility, and an aversion to greed, envy, and other unattractive qualities... A friend of mine says when hiring he looks for three things: intelligence, energy, and character. If they don't have character, the other two traits will kill you because if you hire someone with poor character, you better hope they are dumb and lazy because if they are smart and energetic, they will get you into all kinds of trouble.

At the heart of building *Champions for Life* is the deliberate inculcation of positive values to create strong character. Authentic leaders are always those with high moral character. The Greek philosopher Heraclitus asserted: "A person's character is their destiny." For adolescents and adults, character doesn't make a modest difference; it makes all the difference. Even as a teenager George Washington understood personal character development was imperative: "In all my endeavors I have sought to make fitness of character my primary objective." Among the Founding Fathers there were at times many bitter differences and rivalries. The Father of our Country was the exception. He was the one leader that no one harbored negative feelings toward because he was universally admired for his sterling character. From paragons like Washington, we are reminded that in the prioritization of core values that will guide our development, attention to character ought to supersede everything except faith. Character even trumps education. As Teddy Roosevelt remarked: "To educate a man in mind, but not in morals, is to educate a menace to society."

Today, there is a tragic shortage of people in our society with unflinching morals including, sadly, people in leadership positions. This void can easily be observed in lives ranging from government officials to Wall Street charlatans, from fast-food employees to professional athletes, and even Little League coaches and teachers. You have to think long and hard to identify high profile leaders worthy of emulation today. Contemporary newspaper and tabloid headlines often spotlight spectacular ethical failures. Contrast that by turning back the clock 240 years to our country's founding when 90% of everything taught in all our schools was of an ethical, moral, or religious nature and a different picture emerges. Out of a population of only three million in those 13 colonies, titans such as Washington, Adams, Franklin, Paine, Madison, Marshall, Jefferson, Hamilton, and many others arose. It was once understood that sound moral principles and character were intended to be at the core of our nation. Today, with a population of 300 million, we have trouble naming two or three contemporary leaders we genuinely admire. Building character today is given short shrift compared to padding resumes, solidifying stock portfolios, or increasing fame. This is due in part to the fact that the formation of stellar character is anything but easy. Few can explain the difficulty of doing this in life better than Helen Keller:

Character cannot be developed in ease and quiet, only through experience of trial and suffering can the soul be strengthened, vision cleared, ambition inspired, and success achieved. Silver is purified in fire and so are we. It is in the most trying of times that our real character is shaped and revealed.

Adults have the responsibility and privilege to guide young people *through* the fire, not to avoid it or to be consumed by it. For young people, a life of ease can lead to a lifetime of dis-ease. So many parents and adults today do not understand the crippling effects of protecting and rescuing adolescents from hardship at the sacrifice of principle. Conversely, steady sacrifice for a cause greater than ourselves, in a disciplined environment, produces an honor that cannot be bought or sold, traded or stolen. As a country, we have erroneously assumed for too long that strong character "just happens" and is acquired naturally, without any proactive training or discipline. Because of our indifference to fortifying this pillar needed for a strong society, we find ourselves in dire straits, desperately thirsting for more people of high character and integrity but unwilling ourselves to commit to the principles and disciplines that create that character and integrity. As a coach, Jim always believed that, "you win with character, and you lose with characters."

Rising unemployment, burgeoning deficits, and growing despair are the hallmarks of America's pandemic and economic dilemma. Numerous articles have been written about the mechanistic flaws in our capitalistic system, but few identify some of the prime sources that produce recurring economic debacles. Discussions center on the disastrous effects of COVID-19, credit defaults, government over-regulation, stagnant industries, and a host of other legitimate problems. What are less scrutinized are the internal character traits that spawned these nightmares with the exception of the pandemic. Yet those character flaws are widespread and can be found in all strata of our society; Republican, Democrat, rich, poor, black, white, Wall Street, and Main Street. Avarice, comfort at all costs, and a "something for nothing" culture have made their insidious way into our society's bloodstream.

The root cause of the systemic cultural crisis we are currently struggling with in this country has less to do with the economy or health care system or tax system than with the decline in American character. The only sure way to fix it for the long term is to build generations of workers and leaders -citizens- who value honesty over expediency, service over self-centeredness, and civility over crudeness. In journalist Tom Brokaw's inspiring book, *The Greatest*

*Generation*, he describes a well-spring of men and women who came of age during the Great Depression defending the world from the Nazi regime and the Empire of Japan. These were young people who chose to humbly place God and country above their own lives, making the sacrifices to defeat tyrannical and diabolical forces of darkness. They were also a hard-working, self-sufficient generation, expecting no one to take care of them while generously helping others. What sometimes is forgotten in pouring out deserved lavish praise upon this heroic generation is the noble efforts of parents of inculcating great values in them. That legion of remarkable parents did an incredible job of instilling the virtues which would carry a country to greatness. Today, as leaders, we are tasked with a similar objective, to raise up a new "Greatest Generation" equipped to overcome the monumental challenges that will besiege us in the future. This indispensable goal, the deliberate development of character, produces values-based victories which regularly triumph in both personal and public lives and can restore our culture's viability. When the common theme appearing in the honor codes at our service academies, "A cadet will not lie, cheat, or steal, or tolerate those who do" becomes the modus operandi at all our schools and universities, we will spark a character revival capable of producing large numbers of championship caliber people. This character resurgence effort must be focused on our youth. Former Nebraska Athletic Director Tom Osborne explained:

> Dallas Cowboys' Coach Tom Landry often said he could not recall changing the character of even one of his pro players… Because their character had been fully developed by the time they got to the NFL… Players entering a college football program are younger and we [college coaches] were able to affect some change… However, even by age 18, their basic character had been molded and dramatic change was rare.

General Douglas MacArthur once remarked that failure in war was attributable to two words: "Too late." Emphasizing the paramount importance and urgency of outstanding character traits and virtues among our children and adolescents is the only sure-fire cure for what is ailing America today. *Champions for Life* can only be developed by leaders who themselves embrace the core principles outlined in this book.

A person's character is the content of their heart. It is the inner substance of who we are manifested through our choices and actions - the triumph of convictions and commitments over temptations and excuses. Ben Franklin once remarked, "I never knew a man who was good at making excuses who was good at anything else." Good character is the foundation for trust between people, and what permits us to work together productively without destroying each other. The actual derivation of the word "Character," from the Greek which means "to engrave," indicates to us the strenuous process a person undergoes to acquire strong character. We typically think of engraving as a specialized metal or woodworking skill performed by expert craftsmen. It is similar with people; it takes a skilled mentor to weave crucial values into the fabric of our beings. Good character is not an inherent gift, but something that must be constructed brick by brick. The engraving of values such as honesty, respect, determination, honor, and courage is an ongoing process that is never completed. Even as mature adults, we never reach the character "finish line" because our hearts literally have unlimited capacity for deeper engravings of positive values.

The other often overlooked aspect of good character is its orientation toward action. Here it is vital to distinguish between a moral person and a person of character. Morality centers on not doing something which is wrong whereas character is having the courage to proactively do that which is right. Dr. Martin Luther King struck at the heart of this difference when he said:

> You may be 38 years old as I happen to be. And one day, some great opportunity stands before you and calls upon you to stand up for some great principle, issue, or cause. And you refuse to do it because you want to live longer or you're afraid you'll lose something of value to you, or that you'll be ridiculed or criticized. Well, you may go on living until you're 90, but you're just as dead at 38 as you would be at 90. And the cessation of your breathing is but the belated announcement of an earlier death of the spirit. You died when you refused to stand up for truth and justice.

Dr. King was admonishing the moral bystanders, the "good people," in the struggle for civil rights and justice. He does not question their morality, because they know the difference between right and wrong; he does, however, challenge them to display righteous character, by putting their morality into practice. In examining the history of the world, it has always been the faith and character of a small group of people like The Founding Fathers and Jesus' Disciples who have changed the world. Inspirational character comprises the values engraved on our hearts and the willingness to put these virtues into action regardless of the personal cost.

Character formation begins with parents, teachers, and coaches who all play seminal roles in "engraving" core values onto the hearts of children. In athletics, there is an old saying that "sport doesn't teach character, coaches do." Regardless of any sport's perceived intrinsic value, it is the leaders of teams who must accept the responsibility and seize the opportunity to use their sport or activity as a vehicle to teach larger life lessons – to instill principles and habits that extend far beyond the playing field or gym. To hope that a young person will acquire noble traits through haphazard guidance is wishful thinking. Why? Just as weather can erode carvings over time, internalized values can dissipate. In fact, the Apostle Paul, in 1 Corinthians 15:33, wisely and succinctly warns: "Bad company corrupts good character." There are countless examples in life when associating with the wrong crowd following corrupt leaders has destroyed a potentially strong and positive character. Perhaps no tragedy captures this truism better than the following story of brothers Edwin and John.

In 1833, Junius and Mary Booth gave birth to a son by the name of Edwin. They loved their son very much and provided a nice home for him, including the privilege of attending excellent private schools as a boy. Five years later Edwin's brother John was born into the same home, receiving the same attention, love, support, and education. Both Edwin and John followed in their father's footsteps by becoming successful stage actors. Edwin lived a very productive life before dying in 1893 at the age of 60. Unfortunately, John's life took a far different turn culminating with his ignominious death in 1865 at the young age of 27. Junius and Mary had tried valiantly as parents to imbue their children with strong values. But John, unlike his brother Edwin and other siblings, fell in with the wrong crowd. The cultivation of strong moral seeds in John's heart fell in shallow soil, never fully sprouted, and were eventually choked out by ill-chosen brethren.

On April 9, 1865 General Lee surrendered to General Grant at Appomattox signifying the end of the tumultuous Civil War. Two days later on April 11, President Abraham Lincoln gave a speech at the White House articulating his vision for a united country where increased freedoms for everyone, including the right of former slaves to vote, were enumerated. Unfortunately, John was in the crowd that day. Hearing Lincoln's declaration of rights for newly emancipated slaves enraged him. He vowed menacingly in response: "Now by God! I'll put him through. This is the last speech he will ever make!" Three days later on April 14, 1865, John Wilkes Booth made good on his threat, assassinating President Lincoln while he was watching a play at Ford's Theater.

Junius and Mary Booth never dreamed while bouncing young John on their knees he would one day be hunted like an animal as the most wanted man in American history. The Booth's dinner conversations with the children during their formative years never prepared them for the devastating news that their family name would one day be ruined in the wake of the murder of America's most beloved leader. While there are multiple reasons John Wilkes Booth pulled the trigger on that fateful day in Washington, no one can deny there was an absence of high moral fiber in the assassin.

A person's legacy will always reflect their character first, and achievement second. That is why quality organizations are so focused on attracting and hiring people with the highest quality character. Former Super Bowl coach Tony Dungy said there were only a couple of factors that could remove a college football player from consideration for his NFL team, the key one being character. This goes against the "get results quick" approach that expediently covets talent above character, where a player's gifts outweigh his substance. For character-based organizations, serving the right ends by utilizing the right means is the only acceptable approach. For individuals, cultivating and nurturing strong character is a foundational task. A strong and unwavering character in individual lives is critical to build and sustain enduring and genuine success in any organization today.

Role models like Coach Dungy clearly understand there are moral laws of nature which govern our universe and the neglect or defiance of these will wreak havoc, just as there are physical laws which can only be ignored at our peril. The economic crisis of recent years, sparked largely by the collapse of the subprime mortgage market, was engineered primarily by Wall Street firms who rationalized that amassing vast wealth while building a house of cards was a sustainable enterprise or, if not sustainable, at least lucrative enough to justify actions devoid of character. At the other end of the catastrophe's spectrum, many loan recipients deluded themselves into believing there would be no day of reckoning for seeking to get something of substantial value for little sacrifice. The laws of economics, or the laws of physics, are identical to the moral laws that govern our personal lives in significant ways. If we step off the edge of a skyscraper, the law of gravity plunges us to our demise. To defiantly oppose those obvious physical laws is a supreme act of foolishness. Similarly, Richard Nixon and Bill Clinton suffered very painful and embarrassing consequences when they stepped off the 'moral ledge.' To avoid being central figures in our own self-made Greek tragedies requires a recognition of, and commitment to, wisdom and principles which produce rock-solid character. Professor Cornelius Platinga of Calvin College describes scriptural wisdom as the "knowledge of God's creation and the knack of fitting oneself into it." This comprehension of the moral and spiritual Laws of Nature is what scripture calls "wisdom."

To become a person of wisdom and integrity is life's most important goal. Integrity is derived from the Latin - *integritas*, which means 'whole, entire, complete.' Mathematicians derive the word 'integer' from this same Latin root to describe a whole number. A person of *integrity* is a 'complete or whole' individual who has a pyramid of values drilled into their core being. At the center of our character must be a value that serves as the building block for all others. If it is missing, the pyramid will eventually collapse in ruin. This value is *honesty*. Experiences in life prove that if this core value is absent, someone will eventually get hurt. At the turn of the century, Marion Jones was one of America's sweethearts known for her athletic prowess in winning three gold medals and two bronze medals in Sydney, Australia. Following the Olympic Games, Jones condescendingly wagged her finger in the faces of the press as she chastised them for accusing her of using steroids. However, seven years later Marion Jones tearfully met the same members of the press, and millions of fans who had supported her, and apologized admitting she had used steroids in her quest to become the "greatest female athlete in the world." The value of honesty had somehow taken a back seat in her race for fame and acclaim, with disastrous consequences. The absence of this value cost Marion Jones her five medals, millions of sponsorship dollars, and six months in prison. Her reputation was shattered and she faced an uphill climb of mountainous proportions to rebuild her character.

It is sad to see high profile athletes, movie stars, and other public icons fall from glory because of character flaws. It is even more devastating when national political or economic leaders lack strong values. David Gergen, who has served as an advisor to four U.S. Presidents, senior political analyst for CNN, and professor at Harvard University, bluntly asserts that "Character without capacity usually means weakness in a leader, but capacity without character means danger." Many people have the capacity or talent to lead, but lack the character to positively shape the lives of others. In the long run, leadership effectiveness in life hinges most critically on *who* you are at your core. Only when a leader has a formation of strong character can his or her talents be put to their purpose and highest use.

Character education is a lifelong endeavor. Inculcating strong values into the hearts of today's children is the most important responsibility that parents, teachers, and coaches must embrace. Aristotle succinctly reminds us that "Educating the mind without educating the heart is no education at all." There is great relevancy and urgency in character education, as events in our war on terror have reminded us. On September 11, 2001 the world watched in horror as a few diabolical Muslim extremists brought evil to the United States, brutally slaughtering some 3,000 innocent people. Mayor Rudy Giuliani, as leader of one of the world's most powerful cities, strategically mobilized thousands of brave heroes to tend to the devastation, and to the dead and injured innocent citizens. Giuliani received great praise for his leadership during those shocking and tragic days in American history. The framework for his successful crisis management lay in his personal credo: "You've got to build yourself up for the terrible things that are going to happen so that your response to them will be routine." Time invested in preparation before traumatic events occur is a real key to success. But not all possible events can be anticipated and prepared for. Instead, it is the embracing of strong core values and unwavering commitment to personal character that prepare us best to deal with the unexpected and the difficult. It is character preparation that is critical. NBA Orlando Magic senior Vice President Pat Williams contends, "You must prepare yourself ahead of time in order to maintain your character and integrity when temptation comes." Investing in etching deep positive values will yield the strength to overcome the inevitable temptations and challenging events we will face throughout our lives. Hence, fortifying strong values in our lives today is a daily obligation, a daily discipline. It begins with the books we read, the media we are exposed to, and the people we interact with. If you put on a pair of white gloves but then rub them in the mud, you'll always have mud-stained gloves, unsuited for the intended tasks. So it is in life when we choose to allow our minds and hearts to be infected with the baser temptations of this world. Billy Graham was right when he commented that "the only thing that happens when you wrestle with a pig is that you both get muddy." That is in part why the Apostle Paul encourages us in Philippians 4:8, "Finally friends, whatever things are true, noble, lovely, and of good report, if there is any virtue and anything praiseworthy, think on these things."

Ultimately for our country there is no simple or easy political or economic solution to our present quagmire, which is headlined by the acrimony and incivility we daily witness in Washington DC. Even the historically peaceful and smooth transition between presidential administrations came under siege after the election of Joe Biden. The only sustainable way out of our present culture wars is through a reawakening and cultivation of timeless principles that yield honorable character. This is a lifelong process of commitment and discipline. So often we avoid facing the simple, but hard solutions to our most vexing problems as the following humorous story illustrates:

> In ancient Babylon, one day the king summoned all his wisest counselors. He instructed them to record the most important laws and principles that should govern their empire. One year later, the scholars returned with a

three-volume treatise containing several thousand pages covering what they believed would fully describe the most exemplary behavior and principles that should be strived for and abided by. The king smiled and told them it was far too long and detailed. Six months later the scribes returned with a 100 page document. No, the king told them, it was still too cumbersome. Disappointed, but undaunted, the wise counselors set out to further distill their findings. After another six months, they presented the sage king with a 10 page summary. Again the ruler complimented them on their effort but said they had still not reduced it to its most essential. Finally, three months later, they returned to their sovereign with a single sheet of paper that bore a one sentence declaration, "There's no such thing as a free lunch!" The king beamed his approval and exclaimed, "Now you've got it!"

Good, honorable character is the one sentence solution we need today. But there is no easy or quick path to rock solid character. We have deluded ourselves into believing there is a "free lunch" that everyone in our society deserves. In the mid-2000s, Wall Street financiers packaged worthless, and even fraudulent, sub-prime loans into securities they sold worldwide. Main Street folks sought low to no interest loans, pretending there would be no day of reckoning. Thinking we have the freedom to enjoy and consume without responsibility is a recipe that will eventually exact a heavy toll, and we are paying a steep price now in our country as a result of ignoring that important principle.

Chuck Colson, in his insightful book, *How Now Shall We Live,* discusses the importance and relevance of "worldview" to character and our lives. Each person, whether they recognize it or not, operates according to a worldview, which is a way of understanding and viewing all areas of life and thought, both the physical and the moral. He clarifies for us that worldviews fall into one of two distinct categories - one recognizing God at its center and the other based on random chance.

As we seek to build *Champions for Life*, do we view our lives and the lives we seek to equip and empower as distant relatives of some shiny sea organisms that haphazardly evolved or as the children of a loving and merciful God. When poor behavioral choices are made, do we view them as understandable behavior of struggling organisms engaged in the survival of the fittest, whose natural impulses center around survival and gratification, or as transgressions of God's laws which cry out for redemption? Russian writer Boris Pasternak wrote "We have to understand our attitude toward existence, our place in the universe. Otherwise, life is meaningless. This means a rejection of a materialistic worldview and a resurrection of our interior life, a resurrection of religion."

The most successful shapers of history have been transformational leaders with impeccable character. They have, through heroic acts of service and sacrifice guided by core principles and strong character, transformed the interior lives of people. Pastor Andy Stanley defines character as "the will to do what is right, as defined by God, regardless of personal cost." Jesus transformed us from unacceptable to righteous in the eyes of God through the sacrifice of being nailed to a cross. Martin Luther King, Jr. helped transform us into a more just and caring society by appealing to core principles of justice and capturing the hearts of the righteous. Mother Teresa transformed the "hopelessly suffering" to the "dignified hopeful" despite unimaginably dire living circumstances through the application of core Biblical principles. Theodore Roosevelt boldly said it, as he lived it, "Character, in the long run, is the decisive factor in the life of an individual and of nations alike."

Once the proverbial rudder on the ship of our lives is secured, leaders must not only model good character for others they impact and influence, but also create and execute a deliberate plan for inculcating it. In Jim's football program, 15 minutes a day before practice is devoted to character and leadership training with his players. Virtues such as integrity, honesty, service, determination, courage, resilience, forgiveness, commitment, honor, and loyalty are discussed. Stories are often used as the medium through which these values are shared. The expectation for student athletes is always that these virtues are to be practiced with just as much focus as proper techniques are for the respective football positions they play. Even more importantly, the practice of these attributes is encouraged and expected off the field and in their homes. At the end of practices, players are often reminded to live these virtues when they get home by immediately proactively helping a parent or family member, usually their moms, with any chores or assistance they may need. Players are also taught to greet others properly with respect and deference when appropriate, to look others in the eye, and to firmly shake hands. They address adults with respect by using their titles and saying sir and ma'am whenever appropriate. If they see someone alone at break or lunchtime, or simply in need of some kind of help, they are taught to reach out and offer company or assistance. These are not actions encouraged to make them look good, but rather the consequence of hearts and minds with an upward and outward focus rather than inward absorption. Central to being a contributing member to a good team, whether that team is a family, business, or any other type of organization, is learning to surrender to a greater cause and sacrificing for others that brings out the best virtues in us. In this particular case, football is the vehicle through which good virtues are transmitted, nurtured, and practiced. The commitment to living principle-centered lives where good character is consistently radiated is one of the chief hallmarks of any group or organization committed to making a positive difference in our society. And placing God at the center of our lives is the essential galvanizing factor which produces strong character to become *Champions for Life*!

# "Champions Forge Strong Character"
## *Championship Points*

1. The heart of a *Champion for Life* is engraved with positive values.

2. The greatest individual goal in life is to become a person of wisdom and integrity.

3. Building character is an intentional process.

4. Character is destiny.

5. Delaying or ignoring character development is to court disaster.

6. Talent and intellect minus character is dangerous.

7. Legacy is foremost a reflection of character.

8. When adversity strikes it is too late to form character.

9. Leaders focus more on how to **be** than how to **do**.

# Chapter 3
## "Champions Reflect Humility"

*"The best leaders are usually humble leaders because they gain loyalty through respect rather than bravado."*

*(John Wooden)*

Jesus, the incomparable leader, lived His life giving a consistent testimony of many virtues etched into His core as He left an indelible mark on everyone He met. There is one time when Jesus clearly drew attention to two attributes of His character which we should note as we strive to become *Champions for Life*. In Matthew 11:28-29 Jesus said, "Come to me all you who are weary and burdened, and I will give you rest… for I am *gentle* and *humble.*" These two characteristics have become increasingly rare in our society as our culture encourages and even celebrates abrasiveness, brashness, and arrogance in today's dog-eat-dog world. But ask yourself, how would your family, team, or business office be enhanced if there were more kindness and humility that permeated the daily grind?

In ancient times, Naaman was a successful Syrian General admired for his battlefield acumen and prowess. But he was also, unfortunately, afflicted with the dreaded disease of leprosy. This mighty man of valor was desperate to be healed. Hearing that a prophet named Elisha might help him, Naaman traveled to Israel. After a long journey, he arrived at Elisha's home expecting the prophet to welcome him lavishly. Instead, Elisha sent a servant to instruct the General to wash in the Jordan River seven times. This infuriated Naaman who was so puffed up with self-importance he expected the prophet would come heal him personally in dramatic fashion. Feeling slighted, the General left upset, too arrogant to heed Elisha's instructions. Only after he had calmed down and listened to a wise servant's advice did he relent and go to the Jordan. There he washed seven times and, just as Elisha had foretold, he was immediately cleansed and cured. Had it not been for the wisdom of a humble servant, the overly proud and presumptuous warrior would have spent the rest of his life in an agonizing battle with an awful disease. His lack of humility nearly doomed him.

The word humility is derived from the French, meaning "to harness power." It is the antithesis of arrogance, which could be sarcastically described as a strange disease that makes everyone ill except for the person who has it! Humility is an invaluable virtue for many reasons. The humble person recognizes their need for a saving God, realizing that their shortcomings create a barrier between them and the perfect Creator. This humility helps drive us to our knees so we stop looking down and look up to the only one who can bridge our imperfection gap.

Humility is not about denying our positive attributes or achievements, it simply redirects our focus to recognize the positive in others. Proverbs 27:2 says, "Let another praise you, and not your own mouth, someone else, and not your own lips." Solomon's wise advice underscores another biblical truth, "humility precedes honor." We rob ourselves of the possibility of godly honor when seduced by the glories of our own status, possessions, or achievements.

Genuinely humble people don't engage in false modesty; that is, they don't deny their authority, talents or knowledge, but they do recognize that the source of their power or blessings doesn't emanate from within themselves. They have a stewardship mentality, understanding that all they treasure are precious gifts from God to be used not only for their own needs and enjoyment, but in service to others and for enriching and expanding His Kingdom.

Humble people instinctively give respect and esteem to others. The humble command respect, they don't demand it. A good leader knows that everyone is valuable, but also that no one is indispensable. A poem which Jim's high school coach taught to him as a thought for the week expresses well the delusions that the haughty have with their own indispensability:

*The Indispensable Man*

Sometime when you're feeling important;
Sometime when your ego's in bloom

Sometime when you take it for granted
You're the best qualified in the room.

Sometime when you feel that you're going
Would leave an unfillable hole,
Just follow these simple instructions
And see how they humble your soul;

Take a bucket and fill it with water,
Put your hand in it up to the wrist,
Pull it out and the hole that's remaining
Is a measure of how you'll be missed.

You can splash all you wish when you enter,
You may stir up the water galore,
But stop and you'll find that in no time
It looks quite the same as before.
The moral of this quaint example
Is do just the best that you can,
Be proud of yourself but remember,
There's no indispensable man.

Humility fuels an appetite for learning and improvement. It naturally epitomizes the Japanese concept of "Kaizen," the process of continuous improvement. When we recognize the truth in former Notre Dame Football coach Lou Holtz's insight that "the biggest room in the world is the room for improvement," we set ourselves on an exhilarating path of adventurous possibilities. Nowhere in the history of college football is this practical wisdom more evident than at Kansas State University, where legendary Coach Bill Snyder engineered the greatest turnaround in collegiate gridiron history beginning in the late 1980s. Coach Snyder explained that they achieved that remarkable feat by focusing their players on "finding a way every day to become a better person, student, and athlete." He did this by teaching and constantly reinforcing what he called "The 16 Wildcat Commandments." These were a set of virtues, expectations and goals that helped focus each player and staff member on pursuing championship excellence without deviation. The net result of inculcating the 16 Commandments was a culture that pursued greatness on a daily individual and corporate basis.

One season, just four days before the Lancer's opening football game, Jim received a phone call from a concerned parent of one of his players. The father shared with Jim he had found marijuana in his son's room. After confronting him, his son admitted use, explaining he had gotten it from another player. This was troubling in and of itself, but it also had serious ramifications for the Lancer team. An athletic policy was in place stating those who used drugs or alcohol received an automatic 30 day suspension from participating in games. This meant, if true, these two players would miss the first four games of the season. In questioning the boys, to their credit, they confessed but in the process also shared concerns about two other players. To make a long story short, 15 players were suspended three days before opening kickoff for either alcohol consumption or marijuana use. Seven players were starters. In the age of the internet, sports controversies surface quickly, and sure enough Jim received phone calls from reporters shortly after the first game when it was noticed that several starters were missing. Without sharing details, Jim confirmed that 15 players were suspended for rules violations. Jim reiterated that while all young men were of special value to the team, the only things that are indispensable are the principles we live by. To raise *Champions for Life*, we must ingrain in our people the pricelessness of the timeless values we willingly and humbly subordinate ourselves to. Humble people recognize the need for accountability in their own lives and for the people they serve. Conversely, to withhold accountability for expediency's sake undermines the foundation necessary for an honorable life. By the way, despite missing those key starters, the Lancers won those four games against four talented and highly ranked opponents. And three of those victories were won in the closing seconds against very daunting odds!

Rick Warren's transformational book, *The Purpose Driven Life*, begins with a simple riveting reminder: "It's not about you." As *champions* and leaders, where we focus our time, talents, and treasure will depend much on whether we have humble hearts which are upward seeking and outward serving, or whether we are conned or deluded into thinking, "It's all about me." Humility gives leaders the genuine authority to serve and create followers through personal influence. Those lacking a humble spirit rely on their position or title to force or coerce others to do their bidding. The biggest problem with this is that over time it erodes relationships and diminishes effectiveness. Conversely, the humble have staying power. When you think of the greatest, most influential leaders, our fondness and respect for them centers as much on their humility as on their actual abilities and deeds. For most, humility was a driving force at the heart of who they were and what they did. A simple truism of life worth remembering is: arrogance is repulsive while humility has a charismatically attractive quality about it.

Humility is an invaluable virtue as exemplified by the story of the Roman Centurion who approached Jesus, beseeching Him to help his dying servant. A Centurion was a Roman officer in command of 100 soldiers. Generally, they were promoted to the level of Centurion because of proven valor and leadership skills. They had a commanding bearing and their presence was typically feared among subjugated peoples, such as the Jews in Galilee. It was in the Galilean town of Capernaum that the Centurion humbly sought Jesus. He immediately referred to the carpenter from Nazareth as "Lord," which must have been shocking to those witnessing a Roman Commander behaving deferentially toward a "conquered peasant." He then requested Jesus' help in healing his servant, who was back at his home lying in tormented paralysis. Jesus offered to go right away to tend to the servant, but the Centurion said it wouldn't be necessary for two reasons: (1) the Centurion said he was not worthy of having the Lord enter his home; and (2) he stated that if Jesus merely "spoke a word," even without seeing the ill servant in person, that the servant would be made well. It is a compelling display of the deepest humility and faith which Jesus recognizes and honors by replying: "I have not found such great faith, not even in Israel….. Go your way; and as you have believed, so let it be done for you." The servant was healed that same hour.

The Centurion is a powerful model of the two most vital elements of servant leadership. First, his leadership and character were rooted in a self-effacing modesty that recognized the existence and authority of God. Second, he focused on serving the needs of those placed under his command, intuitively understanding that authority is a privileged responsibility given to leaders by God to help others. His unflinching faith reflected St. Augustine's description of the power of belief: "Faith is to believe what you do not see; the reward of this faith is to see what you believe." What a celebration must have ensued upon the Centurion's return home to his healthy servant! And what prayers of humble thanksgiving must have been received in heaven that day! All because of the Roman Commander's humility and faith.

Is there any greater example of humility than Mother Teresa? This devoted and compassionate servant was a saintly example of Christ-centered charity who became one of the 20th century's most towering tributes to "agape" love. Agape is one of the Greek words for love, conveying giving without an expectation of something in return. John Wooden encouraged us to remember: "[Our] greatest joy definitely comes from doing something for another, especially when it is done with no thought of something in return." President Harry Truman summarized the power of humility as he reminded Americans "It is amazing what you can accomplish when you don't care who gets the credit."

Who can forget the poignant act of humility demonstrated in a collegiate softball game in 2009? With two runners on base and two strikes against her, Sara Tucholsky of Western Oregon University hit her first home run of her college career over the center field fence. Unfortunately, while running the bases Sara missed first base and in returning to tag the base tore the anterior cruciate ligament in her knee. After crawling back to first base in excruciating pain, the umpire told her she would be called out if her teammates tried to help her. The opposing first baseman, Mallory Holtman from Central Washington, then asked the umpire if she and her teammates could carry Tucholsky around the bases with no penalty to her. The umpire affirmed this would cause no penalty to the opposing player or team. So Holtman and shortstop Liz Wallace picked Tucholsky up and carried her around the bases, stopping to let Tucholsky touch each base with her non-injured leg. This humble act of compassion by these two players from Central Washington allowed Tucholsky to enjoy her first career homerun and her team's 4-2 victory which ended Central Washington's chances of winning the conference and advancing to the playoffs. This story shows how elevating principles of sportsmanship, fairness, and caring of others above personal interests is an extreme act of humility treasured and remembered.

One of the turning points for Kent's Concordia University Irvine women's basketball program occurred on an ordinary day when the team was broken into two groups to compete in a shooting drill. Most coaches know that instilling competition in practice drills heightens concentration and effort. The incentive used to intensify the competition is usually that the 'losers' run extra while the 'winners' enjoy a respite and get to watch their teammates run. On this day, the losing team was on the line ready to run, and just before the whistle was blown to begin the painful running, one of the "winners" got on the line to run with her teammates temporarily labeled as "losers." This additional running by one of the "winners," this act of humility and shared effort did not go unnoticed by all in the gymnasium. As a coach, Kent almost put a stop to this one athlete needlessly punishing herself, but he realized there might be something bigger happening here than he had ever witnessed in his years as an athlete or coach. To his pleasant amazement, the next time a losing group was assigned extra conditioning, the same athlete was joined by the rest of the 'winners' on the line, who collectively ran with their teammates. Kent observed how humility and gentleness are contagious characteristics within a group. To this day he is confident that the Concordia Eagle basketball team enjoyed two trips to the NAIA National Championship Tournament in 1992 and 1993 for a variety of reasons, but none more critical than the team's sense of cohesion derived from the selfless tone of humility set that one day by a 'winner' on the line with the 'losers.'

When you analyze some of the world's most revered leaders, you will find a deep sense of humility etched into their hearts. General George Washington, when notified that he was selected to lead the colonists against the daunting British army, politely accepted the nomination with these words:

> I beg they [Second Continental Congress] will accept my cordial thanks for this distinguished testimony of their approbation. But lest some unlucky event should happen, unfavorable to my reputation, I beg it may be remembered by every gentleman in the room that I this day declare with the utmost sincerity I do not think myself equal to the command I am honored with.

Abraham Lincoln exhibited great humility after enduring severe adversity in his life prior to becoming our nation's 16th president. President Lincoln is recognized as a leader who spent more time outside of his office than any other president, humbly visiting and encouraging those who served with him. Lincoln could have remained cocooned in the safety and comfort of the White House during the dangerous days of the Civil War; however, he knew he was elected by the people to serve them, not to be sequestered from them. Other peace activists like Martin Luther King Jr. and Nelson Mandela exuded a rare sense of humility and love toward others, despite the palpable and intense hostility directed at them. When Mother Teresa died on September 5, 1997 millions mourned her death at the age of 87. This faithful Catholic nun had spent her life humbly holding the dying and feeding the hungry, in one of the most poverty stricken spots on earth in Calcutta, India. Humility in these great leaders is one of the core characteristics distinguishing them from their peers. These unforgettable leaders embody the reality that humility is charismatic while arrogance repels. People are eager to be led by the humble. It is, unfortunately, more difficult today to identify leaders who inspire and attract the masses through their humble service like Washington, Lincoln, King, Mandela, and Mother Teresa did.

Humility begins with the recognition that all that we have is a gift from God. We are encouraged to be so very thankful for all the blessings bestowed upon us because there is a delicate balance in life between times of joy and times of adversity. Life has a way of turning on any of us even when we are doing everything right. Former Texas quarterback Colt McCoy had been training for and dreaming of a chance to lead his Longhorns to a National Championship since his youth. In January of 2010, he lived out this dream as the #1 ranked Longhorns faced the #2 Alabama Crimson Tide in the National Championship game. Colt McCoy had every reason to arrogantly boast about his prowess coming into the game as a Heisman Trophy finalist during his junior and senior years and also as the winningest quarterback in college football history. Colt did not carry himself in a cocky manner because he recognized his athletic success was a gift from God, and there were no guarantees of future accolades. Sadly for Colt, his dream of leading the Longhorns to the championship faded quickly when he suffered a routine hit to his throwing shoulder early in the game that left him numb and unable to play the rest of the game. In the interview after the game, Colt reminded millions of viewers he had learned to trust in God in times of joy and in times of adversity, and that he was thankful for what God had blessed him with. Colt McCoy, despite never winning a championship ring, is a wonderful example of a *Champion for Life,* who exudes a refreshing sense of humility.

# "Champions Reflect Humility"
*Championship Points*

1. Humility harnesses power.

2. Humility attracts rather than repels.

3. Humble people see themselves as stewards rather than owners.

4. The humble have a servant's heart.

5. The humble are eager to learn, improve, and contribute.

6. The humble realize that "it's not about me."

7. The humble assume responsibility and disperse credit.

8. Humble leaders take little, give much.

# Chapter 4
## "Champions Unleash the Power of Purpose"

*"A vision is not just a picture of what could be; it is an appeal to our better selves, a call to become something more."*
(Rosabeth Moss Kanter)

The pounding on the front door was merely the beginning of his family's descent into horror. It was during the dark and gloomy days of war-torn Austria in 1944 that renowned Jewish psychiatrist Viktor Frankl's world was ripped apart as the Nazis herded him and his family off like sheep to the slaughter. The Frankls would never see each other again as the only family survivor of the brutal and lethal concentration camps was Viktor. In his gripping book titled *Man's Search for Meaning,* Frankl describes surviving his hellish experience only because he saw a *purpose* for his life. Frankl shares that the men around him who quit seeing a purpose for their existence would usually be dead within 48 hours. For individuals, purpose is as vital to survival as the air we breathe, and for people within organizations it is also the life blood for the ascent to excellence. A critical responsibility of an outstanding leader is generating a *purpose* that ignites people's passion and appeals to the noblest in their nature. As leaders intentionally focus on their purpose in life they fortify the foundation required for building *Champions for Life.*

Purpose can be divided into two components: vision and mission. Vision is indispensable. Visionary leaders see what is not yet visible to everyone else. Vision paints a future panorama that focuses on what you wish to create. It is a hopeful picture keeping everyone in pursuit of what matters most while appealing to the best in our natures. For coaches, it is the snapshot of how our players practice like, how they perform on game days, what they have achieved by graduation, how they will serve in their communities and churches, and even how they will battle in the mountains of Afghanistan. An inspired vision will focus and crystallize a leader's thoughts into action around the principle of serving the long-term welfare of those placed in his or her path.

Author Pat Williams describes vision this way: "Vision is the ability to make the future happen…it is imagination plus action." Compelling visions invariably have a simple clarity easy to grasp but enormously challenging to fulfill. They require the best from everyone to reach fruition. They are vital for the growth of human beings and for satisfying peoples' natural longing to be a part of something greater than themselves that makes a significant improvement in the lives of others. Teams, families, and organizations committed to pursuing a great vision seldom experience insidious morale problems. Conversely, the Bible warns us in Proverbs 29:18 that "without vision the people perish."

A great example of visionary leadership is the Clemson University Football Program. When Dabo Swinney took the head coaching reins in 2008, the Tigers were an above average program at best. Within a few years however, Coach Swinney's vision began to come to fruition and by 2021 he had led Clemson to two national championships and regular appearances in the elite final four for the college football playoff, a consistency matched only by Coach Nick Saban's Alabama squad. This rise to sustained excellence came about because Coach Swinney had a vision for the Tiger program no one deemed possible and he created a culture, standard, and action plan to match that vision.

A critical virtue of visionary leaders is authenticity. They are true to themselves. They have a vision for their lives which can roughly be divided into four areas: spiritual, moral, personal, and vocational. In Shakespeare's Hamlet, when Polonius advises his son Laertes "This above all: to thine own self be true… Thou canst not then be false to any man," he was in effect saying that if your moral vision calls for you to be honest, dependable, and loyal, then do not betray yourself by being dishonest, inconsistent, and disloyal. If we consider the lives of the greatest servant leaders who ever graced this earth, every one of them had a compellingly clear spiritual and moral vision for their lives to which they remained steadfastly faithful. Coach Wooden embodied that truth: "Throughout my career I did not allow others to make me adopt their standard… my success comes not from championships, but the knowledge that I did everything possible to be the best teacher, coach, and leader I was capable of being." Jesus put it this way, "No one can serve two masters. Either you will hate the one and love the other, or you will be devoted to the one and despise the other. You cannot serve both God and money" (Luke 16:13).

Great leaders commune with dreams of greatness. New York Times Bestselling Author, Dinesh D'Souza asserts that much of President Reagan's greatness "derives in large part from the fact that he was a visionary – a conceptualizer who was able to see the world differently from the way it was. While others were obsessed and bewildered by the problems of the present, Reagan was focused on the future." When Martin Luther King, Jr. stood on the steps of the Lincoln Memorial and shared his vision for transforming America from a color-based to a character-based society, he planted righteous seeds in the depths of honorable peoples' hearts and souls. When Winston Churchill stood practically alone in defiant opposition to Hitler's armies of darkness and proclaimed that Britain would achieve victory regardless of the costs, the spirits of the English soared. On a smaller scale, when Coach Gary Barnett took over a struggling Northwestern University football program in the early 1990s, he presented a new vision for the Wildcats: "We're going to take the Purple to Pasadena. If you can't see the invisible, you can't do the impossible." It was more than audacious to predict that the perennial doormats of the Big Ten would one day be conference champions and compete in the Rose Bowl, but that didn't stop Coach Barnett from boldly casting his vision. Over time, he captured his players' and Northwestern University's hearts, and in 1995 the Wildcats kicked off on January 1$^{st}$ in Pasadena in the Rose Bowl against USC.

Duke Coach Mike Krzyzewski embraced the thrilling challenge of moving a mediocre program to consistent participants in "March Madness" competing for national championships. His vision for achieving competitive excellence revolved around unleashing the power of relationships guided by a set of core, inflexible principles: "communication, trust, collective responsibility, caring, and pride." These five values would form a proverbial fist, powerful and formidable when wielded together.

During our lunch meeting in 2006 with Coach Wooden, we discussed his vision for the UCLA basketball program. He shared that he always taught his players to focus their vision on the "unseen scoreboard," the one that measures a person's heart, their willingness to sacrifice for others, and their commitment to boldly strive toward becoming the best they could be while always placing the team's interest above their own. That is in part why he defined leadership as "Helping others achieve their own greatness by helping the organization succeed." The greatest visions always have at their core the desire to significantly help others, especially by making greatness attainable by all. Great teams always embrace a "win-win" philosophy; that is, by focusing on organizational success individual achievement is enhanced. The unselfishness of an organization like this becomes catalytic. Some people within organizations adopt a "win-lose" mentality where they become threatened by the success of others on their own team. This kind of jealous paranoia prevents an organization from ever reaching their maximum potential. The self-centeredness that permeates these teams produces a leveling, mediocre effect, placing a lid on the desire to achieve and improve. Coach Wooden sagely explains,

> When leaders instill the belief that the opportunity for making great things happen is possible in every job, they have achieved something extraordinary. They have created an organization that fosters and breeds achievers, a superior team filled with people striving to reach their full potential in ways that serve the team. It becomes a force with exceptional power and productivity... personal greatness is not determined by the size of the job, but by the size of the effort one puts into  the job.

The greatest visions focus on maximizing a positive impact on people. The Chinese have a proverb: "If your vision is for a year, plant wheat; if it's for a decade, plant trees; if it's for a lifetime, plant people." The best leaders are in the "people growing business." As you think about the vision for your life and for your organization, it is compelling to remember that sociologists believe even the most introverted person will influence 10,000 others in their lifetime. Our lives are like great rivers, reaching places their sources never know. You could stand at the headwaters of the river representing your life and see its immediate impact, but you cannot see the hundreds of additional miles the 'river' of your life will flow with all its offshoots, tributaries, and streams. This humbling realization heightens the importance of personal stewardship. Whatever we pour into our own headwaters will be carried downstream into the lives of many others. We have a responsibility to keep the pollutants away from ourselves and, by extension, from those we touch downstream.

The precious nature of each life has a magnitude magnificent in scope. The future we want to shape and create should always bear this essential truth in mind. Visions not centered on ultimately making this world a better place by improving and enhancing lives inevitably reveal a hollowness that will fail to stir souls. That's why visionary leaders plant shade trees they know they will never sit under. They selflessly take enormous joy from empowering the dreams of others, even more than fulfilling their own. Athletic coaches would like to be leaders of elite teams *in* their community and state, but it is much more important to be molders of great teams *for* our community and country. While competitors are focused on winning conference and sectional championships, it is far more important to zero in on winning hearts and souls through the cultivation and development of faith and character.

While vision should center on the quest to increase others, a leader's vision must simultaneously be committed to the strategic achievement of excellence. In the October 2004 *Harvard Business Review,* an interesting article by Chan Kim and Renee' Mauborgue appeared describing "Blue Ocean Strategy." The concept behind this innovative thought process is to minimize the attention on competition between organizations and instead maximize efforts to offer something of unique value and quality. "Blue Ocean" organizations or teams are those who look for innovation rather than their "Red Ocean" counterparts who are focused on simply trying to outperform rivals by increasing profits and gaining a larger share of existing markets. In the world of education, it is becoming commonplace for private high schools or universities to compete for students or funding on the basis of the excellence of their sports programs, their academics, and/or their safe and caring environments. Tour Mater Dei's High School campus in Santa Ana, California and you can stroll down Heisman Way and past a wall exhibiting athletic achievements that would be the envy of many Division I universities. At Choate or Philips Exeter on the East Coast, their diplomas are viewed as tickets into the most elite colleges in America. Attempting to compete with such athletic or academic powerhouses on their turf, using their metrics, is an uphill battle in those turbulent Red Oceans. Instead, by creating a vision consistent with a Blue Ocean strategy, your focus can be shifted toward new uncontested areas where competition strengths become less and less relevant. This vision creates new demand rather than trying to carve out a niche in an already saturated market place. As Kim and Mauborgue point out, most Blue Oceans avoid using the competition as a benchmark and instead negate the competition by creating a large jump in value. Kim and Mauborgue use the Model T Ford and Cirque du Soleil as prime examples. Cirque du Soleil invented a whole new circus genre by combining traditional circus aspects with spectacular theatrical performances. This added value literally created a whole new audience, and a new market was formed that as yet is without equal. When the automobile was largely an expensive handmade "toy" for the wealthy, Henry Ford conceived of a way to mass produce an efficient automobile at an affordable price and the rest is history.

Being a Blue Ocean visionary and strategist is a potent and compelling asset for leaders. To become a visionary leader requires a person to first allow themselves to be inspired. Trying to lead without inspiration is like trying to drive an unfueled automobile or attempting to generate solar energy on a cloudy day. Inspiration is the energy that helps leaders formulate and live an influential vision to cause change in individuals and throughout organizations. George Barna, founder of *The Barna Group*, a market research firm specializing in studying the religious beliefs and behavior of Americans, defines leadership as "motivating, mobilizing, resourcing, and directing people to passionately and strategically pursue a vision from God that the group jointly embraces." Developing our relationship with God through the Bible, prayer, listening to the wisdom of others, insightful reading, and visiting places of historical importance cultivates the ground that can yield an inspiring vision.

Part of the process of 'visioning' revolves around the concept of "creative tension." Renowned leadership strategist Peter Senge, in his seminal book, *The Fifth Discipline* (1990), discusses the importance of establishing creative tension within an organization. Creative tension is a galvanizing force for positive change and should be embraced. To establish this tension a leader must first carefully assess the *current reality* existing within an organization. Facts are "friends" for those who desire to maximize performance. A leader can gather facts through interviews, surveys, focus groups, analysis of statistics, or simple observation. To bring about positive change, a leader must identify and then articulate the facts to those within the organization. Unfortunately, this is where too many leaders focus all of their attention – on the facts only. Facts by themselves do not motivate or inspire great feats. It is the leader's inspired vision flowing from an accurate assessment of facts coupled with vision, which causes positive change to occur in the lives of those they lead.

In April of 1970, a NASA engineer named Gene Krantz masterfully demonstrated the power of *creative tension* as America faced one of its darkest hours. It was on April 13$^{th}$ when astronaut James Lovell communicated from the Apollo 13 space module 200 thousand miles from earth these fateful words: "Houston, we have a problem." Hundreds of engineers at Mission Control in Houston and millions of Americans realized their greatest fear surrounding space exploration. Krantz immediately mobilized the team of engineers to assess the current reality by analyzing critical facts such as available fuel, oxygen, food, and the location of the Apollo spacecraft. These brilliant problem-solvers provided essential facts and gathered replicas of materials found on the spacecraft. After undertaking a comprehensive review, Krantz passionately inspired everyone in Mission Control with his nonnegotiable vision: "Failure is not an option!" The team embraced the uncompromising passion of their leader. The American space explorers would come home! Astronauts Jim Lovell, Jack Swigert, and Fred Haise were forever thankful for the solutions that arose from the creative tension that occurred in those memorable hours at Mission Control due to the effective leadership of Gene Krantz.

The second component of purpose is <u>Mission</u>. A mission explains the reason for the organization's or team's existence. It explains the "why" for everyone inside or outside your group. It clarifies for all your stakeholders what business you are really in, inspiring commitment to the cause. For Orange Lutheran Football, the mission was simple and clear: "Build Champions for Life." Anything we achieved beyond that became gravy. As successful former CEO of

General Electric Jack Welch comments: "Great organizations are all about finding and building great people." The vision for the Lancer football program was to literally change the world by transforming young lives. The program was anchored in one primary purpose - serving the long-term welfare of the players placed in our care. That was the rudder that steered their ship. In the intensely competitive arena of athletics, we have to decide: Are we going to be Purpose-Driven or Point-Driven (scoreboard)? The paradox we as coaches have both experienced over time is that the greater the attention paid to *purpose*, the more likely a greater number of points will be produced. Substitute *Profits* for *Points* and you are likely to draw the same conclusion in business. Jesus summarized this well in the middle of his Sermon on the Mount when he encouraged us to seek first the Kingdom of God and His Righteousness, and all these other things would be added to us. Some of the most effective coaches such as John Wooden, Tom Osborne, Dabo Swinney, Pat Summitt, and Mike Krzyzweski just to name a few, all placed the greatest emphasis on character development and education, and yet have won substantially and consistently over lengthy periods of time.

Leaders are most impactful when they create a culture of caring while pursuing their mission. They strive to intentionally focus on their personal purpose and, for those they lead, to foster the creation of a culture where the values of caring and excellence converge. These "Twin Towers," of purpose and values become the foundation for building *Champions for Life*. Former Colorado National Championship Coach Bill McCartney believes that the foundation of exceptional leadership lies in the genuine concern for the welfare of others. Jesus taught that all the laws and teachings of all the wisest prophets could be reduced to one simple axiom: Our highest priority should be to love God and love others. The Bible states that God is Love. The three most important forces in our lives according to the Bible are: faith, hope, and love, and the greatest of these is love. We share with our teams that love is the most powerful force in the universe. Here we are not speaking of "love" as an emotional feeling, but rather a serving and sacrificial love defined as the willingness to lay down one's life for a friend. In the riveting account of Navy SEAL Marcus Luttrell in his heart-wrenching book, *Lone Survivor*, Marcus recounts the story of Navy SEAL comrades Mike Murphy, Matt Axelson, and Danny Dietz sacrificing their lives for each other, him, and innocent Afghans, embodying the ultimate testimony of love of laying down their lives for others. Love for others creates a unity which is a powerful *force multiplier* capable of transforming an average organization into an exceptional one.

Outstanding leaders understand that *caring*, *purpose*, and *unity* must all be present to achieve and sustain greatness. Abraham Lincoln had two goals, preserve the Union and end slavery, reflecting a purpose centered on caring about everyone in society while maintaining a unified country at all costs. Lincoln understood the truth in Longfellow's belief that: "All your strength is in your union, all your danger is in discord." In his autobiography, *Long Walk to Freedom*, Nelson Mandela recounted his admiration for an African leader by stating, "He achieved what all great leaders must, he kept his people united." This was President Mandela's greatest challenge when he was elected after 27 years of unjust imprisonment: How to douse the flames of discord fanned by decades of hatred and mistrust? For Mandela, promoting caring-based unity trumped the natural instinct for retribution for the injustices he and the majority of South African people had suffered. Forgiveness was his shield and mercy was his sword, and the transformative power of grace he manifested helped defuse a potentially cataclysmic eruption saving tens of thousands of lives.

Purpose gives us our "Dream Destination." The picture must be clear in our minds. The reason for pursuing the vision must become unequivocal. But that isn't enough. What is often missing is a roadmap that guides us toward fulfilling our purpose. That essential element is *values*. Values are dearly held beliefs about qualities most desirable to us. They delineate what is nonnegotiable, and in the process provide very practical, step-by-step help.

Values serve as the decision makers and template for each issue, choice, and situation a person or organization encounters. In the Orange Lutheran High School football program there were four core values. In order of importance they were:
1. Faith Development
2. Character Formation
3. Educational Achievement
4. Competitive Excellence

Every decision that Jim made, whether it was scheduling opponents, administering discipline, organizing practice, or developing staff, was arrived at through his deliberate subordination to the above values and objectives. They served as the template for Jim, affecting every relationship and funneling each action and decision toward their pursuit and fulfillment.

Values provide leaders clear operational boundaries. Any activity or option that falls outside their realm should not be pursued. Values become tantamount to the straight edges of a puzzle providing boundaries and perspective on which all other decisions are made.

It is vital for a leader to limit the number of core operating values. By lowering the number, it naturally increases the intensity and importance of each value. It is also easier for people to remember three or four values, than to have a vague notion about 20 or 30. Consider the following stellar organizations and the succinct core values that produce excellence:

    * Disneyland: Safety, Courtesy, Efficiency, Show.
    * Nike: Authenticity, Athletic, Performance.
    * In-N-Out Burger: Quality, Friendliness, Cleanliness.
    * Ritz-Carlton: Trust, Honesty, Respect, Integrity, Commitment

The simpler and clearer values are the greater likelihood of their usefulness and ultimate application to achievement. Photographic memories should not be needed for core values to be clearly understood and internalized within an organization.

Values must also be prioritized. The reason for this is simple. They will inevitably come into conflict with one another at various times. Let's say a coach has a player, who is a very diligent student, who seeks to be excused for the first half hour of practice because he needs extra help from his chemistry teacher with an experiment. Because educational achievement is more highly prized than competitive excellence, the player will be granted permission to miss part of practice. Let's say another player asks to miss practice to also receive help from the same chemistry teacher. However, in this case, he is seeking to miss some practice for the extra help because he has chosen not to do his homework and study responsibly. That student-athlete has made poor character choices, and because character formation trumps education, that player will not be given permission to miss. Rewarding poor character behavior is not in anyone's best interest, especially the person who exhibits it. The player will learn in this situation to resume good study habits and not to punish his teammates and coaches by missing practice for avoidable reasons.

The signers of the Declaration of Independence understood prioritization in their life and death quest when they pledged: "Our Lives, Our Fortunes, and Our Sacred Honor." They were willing to sacrifice their lives and lose every penny because their honor, their "Sacred Honor," was where they placed greatest value alongside freedom. Values don't merely indicate what we emphasize in guiding our leadership decisions and choices, they govern our existence.

At the entrance to West Point's football stadium is a plaque with a quote from General Omar Bradley: "I need an officer for a dangerous and secret mission, get me a West Point football player!" Those are exactly the kind of people outstanding organizations are charged with developing - those who can be counted on in the most difficult and challenging of circumstances. The Mission of any great organization boils down to the will, focus, and capacity to unleash the power of purpose to build *Champions for Life*.

# "Champions Unleash the Power of Purpose"

*Championship Points*

1. Purpose ignites passion.

2. Mission clarifies what is relevant.

3. Center your purpose on serving the long term welfare of those entrusted to you.

4. Great leaders look beyond what *is* to what can *be*.

5. Casting an inspirational vision captures hearts.

6. Visionary leaders are "openers of doors."

7. Vision is a snapshot of the future before anyone can see it.

8. Championship leaders serve compelling values.

9. Restrict prioritized core values to no more than four.

10. Core values guide you to your desired destination.

# Chapter 5
## "Champions Focus on Attitude and Effort"

*"The greatest discovery of my generation is that a human being can alter his life by altering his attitudes."*

(William James)

One of the most important principles of servant leadership we have shared with coaches is to never compromise on attitude or effort. The indispensability of choosing to maintain a great attitude which helps sustain an unflagging effort level is underscored in Coach Wooden's Pyramid of Success. Industriousness and enthusiasm are the cornerstones of his Pyramid. An enthusiastic, positive attitude is contagious. Enthusiasm has such a positive connotation in part because it is derived from the Greek *En theos* meaning rooted "in God." The challenge is for leaders to never settle for less than choosing a great attitude.

Recalling the day he was interrogated by the Nazis under piercing lights after being stripped naked, head shaved, wedding ring stolen, and his book manuscript burned, Viktor Frankl describes that in that moment he realized no matter what the Nazis perpetrated, they could not affect his "attitude" without his consent. Frankl discovered a person's attitude is the one freedom that no one can ever take away from you. He experienced the hard way that a person's attitude or outlook on life is neither dependent on genetic predisposition nor environmental factors. Attitude is a "choice" that is made on a daily, sometimes hourly, basis throughout our lives.

Attitude is the way we view or respond to circumstances or events. How important is it? A Stanford study demonstrated that 92% of professional success correlated directly to attitude with only 8% attributable to aptitude. A Harvard study further revealed that 85% of the reason someone acquired, kept, or advanced in a job was attitude, with only 15% traced to knowledge or skills. It is especially empowering to understand that maintaining a great attitude can overcome the most dismal of personal or family circumstances. Condoleezza Rice suggests so many people from around the world continue to be drawn to America's shores because of the "Log Cabin Dream." It doesn't matter where you came from, but rather where you are going, which is driven by your attitude and effort. Dr. Rice is a sterling example herself. As a young African American woman growing up in Birmingham, Alabama she was subjected to the vileness of racism, and yet through sheer determination and discipline rose to the highest levels of government service capped off by her role as the number one diplomat in the world, Secretary of State. Her father had planted the seeds of attitudinal greatness when he taught her, "that she might not be able to have a hamburger at Woolworth's but she could grow up to be President of the United States." While Dr. Rice has not become the President of our country (yet!), she spent a good bit of time at the President's side as Secretary of State and National Security Advisor. Thomas Jefferson was right: "A person with a good attitude can accomplish anything. Nothing can stop a person with the right mental attitude from achieving his goal; but nothing on earth can help the person with the wrong mental attitude."

There are some proactive steps toward developing an attitude of excellence. The first is to feed our minds daily, understanding that input determines outlook. The best way to do this is by beginning each day in an edifying way. Motivational expert Zig Ziglar said he liked to start off each day by reading both the newspaper and the Bible, claiming with a smile that that way he knew what both sides were up to! Leaders cannot give what they do not possess, and great leaders teach out of the "overflow"; that is, they are constantly contributing to others because it steadily flows out from them with a contagious optimism rooted in countless hours of acquiring wisdom.

Greeting people properly is an indicator of an appealing attitude. We teach our students and athletes to shake hands correctly, to address people with respect and proper titles, and to look others in the eye when doing so. When young people greet adults with the deference due their elders, they are honoring timeless principles which help promote civility. Eye contact conveys interest and respect, and increases our ability to not only hear, but truly listen to others. Shaking hands appropriately, creating eye contact, and addressing people respectfully are the keys in the eight or nine seconds we have to make a good initial impression. Margaret Thatcher, former Prime Minister of Great Britain, stated: "I usually make up my mind about a man in ten seconds, and I very rarely change it." An attitude laced with courtesy creates a lasting, positive imprint.

Another way to foster a good attitude is to learn to respond, rather than react. A common mistake made by inexperienced coaches is to overreact emotionally to mistakes made by players. There can be correction and accountability without volatility. This was one of Jim's greatest flaws early in his coaching career, he would overreact rather than take a more thoughtful approach to each situation. Developing the skill of responsiveness helps cultivate the habit of looking for the good in others, recognizing it will cement an attitude of excellence. Steel magnate and philanthropist Andrew Carnegie once remarked that "to find an ounce of gold, you have to mine a ton of dirt." He equated that process to how you lead and deal with people, noting that you don't go into a mine looking for the dirt, but rather the gold in others.

One of the hallmarks of a person who consistently exhibits an outstanding attitude is choosing to live with a thankful heart. Regardless of our circumstances, blessings in our lives need to be recognized and gratefully acknowledged. At the end of each football game, win or lose, the first thing Jim's players do after shaking hands with their opponents is to face the crowd and applaud them. This is a sign of appreciation and respect toward parents, friends, and fans who have generously supported them. Even after a loss, they are like the "Whos" in Dr. Seuss' "The Grinch Who Stole Christmas," who had all their presents taken from them and still gratefully celebrated Christmas morning by bursting into song. Regardless of whether a scoreboard says we won or lost, that should not diminish our "attitude of gratitude" toward Him and those who so richly blessed us.

Leaders should convey an attitude of invincible optimism. Duke Coach Mike Krzyzewski reminds coaches, "Before you ever utter a word, the team sees your face, the look in your eyes, even your walk shows the face your players need to see." Young people and subordinates take their cues from their leaders. Approval, praise, dismay, frustration, exhilaration, hope, disappointment, caring, confidence, belief – all are readily apparent to followers.

Considering this truth, parents and leaders must be self-aware of their attitudinal impact without being self-absorbed. It is imperative for leaders, as Norman Vincent Peale once wrote: "[to] continually practice filling our minds with thoughts of faith, hope, and gratitude, [which] will eventually crowd out our fears."

The essential partner of attitude is effort. Successful people embrace hard work rather than shy away from it. In stellar athletic programs, coaches strive to instill an uncompromising work ethic in their players. Like attitude, this is something that athletes or employees can control. Creating an atmosphere where supreme effort abounds is foundational to success. In his book *Success is a Choice*, Rick Pitino, when he was basketball coach at Kentucky, wrote:

> According to Churchill, victory comes only to those who work long and hard, who are willing to pay the price... Hard work is the basic building block of every kind of achievement... We see our Kentucky team as the hardest working basketball team in America... We try to live up to that standard every day. Are we the hardest working team in America? Who knows? The important thing is we believe it... We believe that all our hard work will enable us to come out on top. Why? Because we deserve it... Success is not a lucky break or a divine right. It is not an accident of birth. Success is a choice.

Nothing shared in this book will lead to success or create a *Champion for Life* without daily effort and discipline. Principles without application get you nowhere. As John Wooden said, "Nothing works unless you do."

There is an entertaining story about Pope John XXIII. Shortly after he was elected Pope, he was showing a visiting delegation of clerics around St. Peter's Basilica in the Vatican. There were many laborers working on restoration projects while many others were milling about. After observing all the workers, one of the visiting clerics asked His Holiness how many people worked at the Vatican? Pope John smiled as it was obvious many laborers were not fully engaged in their tasks and wryly quipped, "Oh, I'd say about half." The visitors laughed. The unfortunate reality is that teams or organizations lacking a high level of industriousness are relegated to perpetual underachievement. As leaders, that failure falls directly on our shoulders. Permitting an environment of substandard effort can be a leader's greatest weakness, and one not easily forgotten. Good leaders embrace responsibility for ensuring the effort thermostat is never set below 100%. Legendary Michigan football Coach Bo Schembechler was a firm believer that the only thing players would struggle forgiving their coaches for would be not pushing them hard enough. In other words, allowing them and their team to become, and achieve, less than what they were capable of.

Not only do champions understand there are no shortcuts to success, but they view hard work as a blessing rather than a burden. There was a saying amongst members of the Greatest Generation: "The hard way is the easy way." So often the siren voices of material comforts, procrastination, entertainment, or the need for instant gratification detour us from the arduous path that raises self-esteem when worthy achievements are realized. Champions never look for the easy way out or the easy path through. They know a lone road leads to the fulfillment of dreams, the one that demands our best, where sweat and honor drip from relentless labor. Heavyweight champion Muhammad Ali told how he hated the endless drain of brutal training sessions, but would refuse to quit because he realized his goal was to "Suffer now and live the rest of [his] life as a Champion." More important, however, than any ring, trophy, or belt that proclaims a person a champion is the character that emerges from an unrelenting work ethic. Historian James Froude captured it this way, "You cannot dream your way into character; you must hammer and forge yourself one."

Attitude and effort are the indispensable fuels of *Champions for Life*!

# "Champions Focus on Attitude and Effort"
*Championship Points*

1. Your attitude is more powerful than your circumstances.

2. Attitude, not aptitude, is the greatest determinant of success.

3. How to develop a positive attitude:
    a. Feed mind daily with edifying input
    b. Greet others with respect and courtesy
    c. Learn to respond rather than react
    d. Cultivate a thankful heart.

4. Achievement depends on effort; hard work breeds success.

5. A positive attitude is contagious, unfortunately so is a negative one.

6. Do not compromise on attitude or effort.

7. Industriousness is a key cornerstone of John Wooden's *Pyramid for Success*.

# Chapter 6
## "Champions are Motivated"

*"Live as if you were to die tomorrow. Learn as if you were to live forever."*

(Mahatma Gandhi)

Apathy abounds! This insidious malady is a pervasive problem affecting every age group, gender, ethnic group, and socioeconomic class. Though the world is full of gifted people, their indifference, sloppiness, and laziness often prevent them from reaching their full potential. Apathetic individuals are at the mercy of others to determine their activity and commitment levels. Teachers, coaches, parents, and CEOs across America wring their hands in frustration as they scramble to motivate others to maximize untapped or underutilized talents. Fortunately, apathy occurs because of a series of poor decisions or an acquired state of mind rather than an unavoidable anomalous genetic condition.

Standing in sharp contrast to apathy are successful people who have an intrinsic drive to make the most of their abilities. Motivated people are self-starters who have the desire to, as John Wooden encourages, "Make each day your masterpiece." Life consistently reveals there is a direct correlation between someone's level of motivation and ultimate success. There are no shortcuts to success, but rather, just a lot of hard work. It may seem trite, but the only place we find *success* in life before *work* is in the dictionary.

Motivation, like apathy, is an acquired characteristic rather than one inherited from our ancestors. If a person is a "self-starter" they have *learned* to embrace this value over time. There is little on DNA strands affecting a person's motivation level outside of providing for general good health. It is perhaps understandable for a person suffering from a debilitating physical condition or chronic illness to struggle with apathy and not to be eager to tap into their potential. Fortunately there are inspiring examples of people like Joni Erickson who show that motivation isn't dependent upon having great health. Joni, became a quadriplegic in 1967 at age 17 after suffering a broken neck in a diving accident. Instead of living a life wallowing in self-pity, Joni learned to paint pictures with a brush in her teeth, wrote over 35 books, and inspired millions through her speeches around the world. Joni's quest to live her life to the fullest is a testament to her high level of motivation and personal resolve to productively enjoy her time and talents on this earth. It is inspiring to see how extreme adversity can bring out the best in a person's character when the right motivation is present.

What is the difference between the self-starter and the apathetic if genetics and overall health are not decisive motivational factors? Motivated people *learn* to adopt a self-starting posture in life at an early age through the influences of their parents, teachers, and peers. According to Albert Schweitzer, leaders must consider that "example is not the main thing in influencing others - it is the only thing." Leadership expert Ken Blanchard believes that the key to authentic, effective leadership is to commit to the process of becoming the person we want to encounter in others. If an individual is highly motivated, they probably grew up surrounded by role models who were highly motivated and influenced them to become self-starters. There is a strong correlation between the motivation level of leaders and their followers. It was keenly apparent when watching legendary coach Pat Summitt conduct practices at Thompson-Boling Arena that her Tennessee Vols had no problem igniting themselves because they were merely reflecting their highly motivated Hall of Fame coach.

Leaders should never underestimate their importance in helping others acquire the foundation that will continually yield high levels of motivation. The quest for excellence is contagious, and once followers understand their leader is committed to excellence they begin their own rise to extraordinary heights. Next to love, believing in others is the most powerful force in the universe. Every player, every young person, every employee deserves a leader who believes in him or her. The most meaningful words in the English language for a leader to share with another person are: "I believe in you!"

A true story illustrating the power of faith and an understanding of just how precious each life is comes from a little 10 year-old boy by the name of Ben Hooper. Ben grew up in the hills of Tennessee in the early 1900s. Ben was fatherless and suffered from the stigma associated with that in those days. One day a new preacher came to Ben's town who quickly developed a reputation for sharing uplifting messages. Lonely and desperate for hope, Ben used to sneak in the back of church to listen and then leave just before the services ended so no one would see him. One Sunday, Ben forgot to exit early and when he finally got up to go he was suddenly frozen in his tracks by the minister's powerful voice booming out, "Boy, hold on just a minute!" Ben stopped as the preacher strode up to him with all eyes riveted on him. The minister looked down at little Ben and asked loud enough for everyone to hear, "Whose boy are you?" Before a quivering Ben could reply, the preacher put his hand on Ben's shoulder, smiled broadly, and said, "Why I know exactly who you are. You, Ben Hooper, are a special child of God. Now you go out in the world and claim your inheritance." Some 30 odd years later, Ben Hooper recalled that that was truly the moment that propelled him to eventually be elected Governor of Tennessee. When a person comes to realize they are a valued child of God it sets them free from the confines of self-doubt and despair. It simultaneously brings clarity to a person's purpose in life, empowering service to others and yielding ultimate fulfillment.

Research indicates that by the time an individual reaches college age, they have established a certain level of motivation that will be similar to that found in their adult years. During these late adolescent years, students are becoming less influenced by the motivation levels of parents and teachers and instead are finding their own personal intrinsic motivation needed for success. Motivation levels are a dynamic daily process where individuals must continually decide to be a "self-starter."

There is a strong relationship between a person's motivation level and their self-discipline, and the eventual success realized in life. Motivation is the ingredient to start someone on a challenge. Without motivation, tasks remain untouched. However, it is ultimately *self-discipline* that provides the framework for getting the job done. Self-discipline fosters strong habits which are necessary to produce success. The goal of leaders then is to teach and instill good habits in followers that will ensure success, and then monitor consistency of effort to solidify high levels of self-discipline.

There are numerous health clubs each January filled with people motivated by New Year's resolutions to lose the unwanted 20 pounds. Alarm clocks go off before sunrise, sending many well-intentioned *motivated* individuals trudging off to the gyms to exercise. However, by early February the lines at the aerobic machines and Nautilus equipment have shrunk because the same "motivated" individuals from January don't have the *self-discipline* needed to realize their weight loss goals. The world is full of individuals who, at one time, are motivated to succeed in every area of life… but fail, due to a lack of self-discipline needed to develop sustainable habits that will build success. From an individual perspective, self-discipline is the most critical key to opening the "Achievement Vault."

There are four ways to motivate people. While all can be effective, two are temporary, yielding only short term benefits. The first of these, incentives or extrinsic rewards, have long been employed by everyone ranging from parents offering an allowance for completing chores, to teachers giving additional grade points for extra credit, to football coaches distributing helmet award decals for big tackles or touchdowns. Salespeople often have clauses written into their contracts promising bonuses based on sales quotas met or exceeded.

The second most basic way to motivate people is primal in nature: fear. Failure to adhere to established standards or meet expectations can cause punishment such as loss of a job, poor grades, or extra conditioning at an athletic practice. Duke Basketball Coach Mike Krzyzewski explains:

> Am I tough on the team? Absolutely. If they don't show respect for the program, for the university, for one another, I'm all over them. I don't want fear to be my primary motivator. But the team has got to know that if they are screwing up, the hammer is going to come down. I'm not going to accept mediocrity at practice.

Jim reminds players at football practices they have full control over their attitude and effort, and that as coaches they will accept nothing less than their best in those two fundamental areas or there will be tough consequences. The critical point is to be careful not to rely too heavily on fear. There is a wise saying that "Regimes planted by the bayonet do not take root."

The other two forms of motivation have much longer lasting potential. The first of these tools employed to energize and enhance performance is establishing goals. Achieving success in life is a process. Successful people set goals as an essential part of that process. This helps individuals become self-starters by focusing daily on whatever behavior is required to meet their goals. Michael Phelps was not surprised in 2008 when eight gold medals were draped around his neck. Phelps stated that he was in the pool for five straight years - 365 days/year - prior to his historic feat at the Beijing Olympics. Success did not surprise Phelps because he had carried out a regimented plan for winning each of those medals for years. Without goals in life, people meander from one task to the next with no direction or connection between their daily tasks and what could occur. Challenging goals heighten motivation and energize determination to put in the work required to reach success.

Dreams are merely that until they are written down on paper and transformed into goals. There is wisdom in setting goals to maximize performance. However, inspirational giant Zig Ziglar reports that 97% of the people in our society do not have itemized goals because they either don't believe they are necessary to achieve success or don't know how to set them. Ziglar describes that it wasn't until he wrote his own personal weight loss goals down on paper, with the obstacles that had previously hindered him from seeing his dream become a reality, that he lost his dangerously high weight. Former Louisville basketball coach Rick Pitino taught his athletes that "Dreams are where we want to end up. Goals are how we get there. Goals are the individual steps we take to ultimately deserve the prize." John Wooden claimed that "instruction works best if it focuses learners on setting and achieving moderately difficult goals which fosters pride in personal accomplishment." Effective leaders know that long-term goals inspire performance today. Goals are our day-by-day blueprints that provide achievable targets for incremental improvement which have the added benefit of helping keep us on track and on time. Leaders do their followers an enormous favor by helping them set concrete and measurable goals to galvanize performance. As coaches we have learned to help athletes set process-oriented goals that focus on personal and team improvement. Former Kansas State football icon Bill Snyder explains process-oriented goals this way: "I have never said our goals are to win a national championship or to rush for so many yards. Our goals have always been intrinsic goals such as improvement every day." Coach Nick Saban's six national championships at the University of Alabama are in part due to the process-oriented goals that are established to create an ongoing culture of excellence.

The most powerful and transformational force in promoting and sustaining motivation is the fourth way: relationships. The following true story is but one small example of millions that convey the atomic capacity of relationships to harness and unleash the best within people. From 1930-1956, Lou Little was a famous football coach at Columbia University, which he led to victory over Stanford in the 1934 Rose Bowl. Before going to Columbia, Lou coached at Georgetown from 1924-1929. While there he coached a 200 pound tackle who, although he tried hard, was not very good. Despite not missing any practices he struggled to improve, and consequently never played. A few days prior to his final game as a senior, Coach Little received a telegram explaining this boy's father had passed away. He knew the father and son had been close, and even remembered them walking around campus arm-in-arm. Lou approached the boy with a heavy heart and after breaking the sad news told him to go home to be with family. Trying to buoy his heart-broken player's spirit he told the boy they would dedicate Saturday's game to the memory of his father.

When game day came, Coach Little was shocked to see the boy standing in the Georgetown locker room suited up ready to take the field with the rest of his teammates. Before Lou could even react, the boy blurted out: "Coach you have to let me start!" Despite his overwhelming compassion for the young man, Lou told him, "This is a championship game. I'm sorry, but I can't take that kind of risk." Without hesitating the boy pleaded, "Coach, I have to do this for my father. Please just put me in for the first play, then you can take me out." Against his better judgment, Lou allowed the boy to run down on the opening kickoff. To his shock and astonishment, the boy flew down the field and made a ferocious tackle, nearly knocking the kick returner out. As he jogged back to the Georgetown sideline, Coach Little waved him back onto the playing field to stay on defense. For the rest of the game, the boy was an unstoppable force. Literally a one-man wrecking crew, the boy led the Hoyas in tackles and on to a victory to secure the Conference Championship.

After the game, a stunned Coach Little asked the young man what had gotten into him. "Coach, there is something you may not have known about my father. He was blind. Today was the first time he ever got to see me play." What lies behind us and before us are of little consequence compared to the power of the love for others that lies within us. Jesus proclaimed, "Greater love has no one than this: to than lay down one's life for one's friends" (John 15:13). Most people will only do so much for money or to avoid a penalty. They will do more in pursuit of a worthy goal. But they will do almost anything, bear any burden, make any sacrifice, for someone they truly respect and care about.

Former Alabama and Georgia Tech Head Football Coach Bill Curry says three elements must be present for relational motivation to occur. "You can't motivate someone unless you care about them, spend time with them, and are honest with them." Zig Ziglar echoed Coach Curry's sentiment as he asserted: "Kids spell love T-I-M-E." Jim often reminds his coaches you can be the greatest technique teacher in the football universe, but if that young man you are coaching doesn't believe you care about him, most of what you try to impart will fall like water off a duck's back. How then do parents, teachers, and coaches most effectively build a relationship bridge with a young person? It begins when we transition into spelling love G-I-V-E. It has been said that the difference between success and significance is when we have a success orientation, we zero in on adding value to ourselves. When we shift toward a significance mindset, our focus becomes adding value to the lives of others. That is what young people, or employees crave in the people they look up to: men and women who have deliberately chosen to lead lives of significance. These leaders create not only an environment of high expectations and accountability where values such as honesty prevail, but care deeply about the welfare of others. This produces a climate of trust, where people can become more than they perhaps ever dreamed. From an athletic standpoint, luck favors teams that trust one another. It is paramount that effective leaders cultivate an atmosphere based on love and unity.

Our experiences as educators and coaches have given us the opportunity to work with some exceptionally talented individuals, and some who have unfortunately not fared so well in life. After reflecting on the differences between the motivated and the apathetic, motivation is ultimately a byproduct of three variables. In any mathematical equation, as the value of each variable increases, so does the product. The formidable challenge of a leader is to raise the value of each variable in the following formula to increase each person's ability to be a *self-starter*:

*Motivation = Expectation x Climate x Value*

**Expectation** refers to the individual's perception of their likelihood of reaching success in what is asked of them. If a teacher asks a student to do something that the student examines and feels there is a "reasonable" chance for success, they will more likely become a *self-starter* and fully engage in accomplishing the task. If the student is being prompted to do something they feel is highly improbable, they will not be so inclined to actively invest their time and energy in carrying out the assignment. A leader's expectations will inspire people to exert concerted effort most especially when they can realistically expect to succeed. Leaders must establish and maintain high standards that demand a commitment to excellence which promotes a healthy pride and confidence. If expectations are low and the task is too simplistic and requires little effort, individuals will lack the desire to invest their time and effort. We have seen poor results from trends in recent years to extravagantly praise and reward children for *unexceptional* results. It is imperative to maintain high standards and challenging goals – for ourselves *and* for those we lead. Coaches know that when their athletes compete against highly ranked teams with great talent, their athletes are much more likely to be highly motivated. Unfortunately, the converse is often true. Playing teams at the bottom of the conference with poor records can lead to a letdown which can cause frustrating upsets.

Leaders must wisely choose tasks for their followers that have challenging levels of rigor. Research indicates the wisdom of establishing an environment of high expectations as people tend to perform to the levels expected of them. It is not a simple process for a leader to set appropriate expectations for themselves and others. The "art" of deciphering what level of expectations to establish is a skill exceptional leaders cultivate through experience, knowledge, and intuition. A key fundamental understanding of effective leaders is that one universal expectation for all people will not motivate equally. The bottom line is, as leaders invest time to strategically establish appropriate expectations for performance, there will be a maximum realization of motivation.

**Climate** is the variable that should be the easiest to control as a leader, but is often overlooked or minimized. If the environment you ask someone to do something in is positive, then individuals will more likely be motivated. Environment refers to the *physical variables* such as comfortable temperature, light, pleasing rooms, useful equipment, and overall positive milieu. There are many students attending schools today in dilapidated classrooms, athletes practicing on rut-filled football fields, employees working in unappealing or poorly designed offices where it should surprise no one that motivation levels wane. A little paint on the walls, clean desks, sod on the fields, and padding on the chairs goes a long way to heighten the desire of people to produce.

Besides the climate's physical factors, there is also the *psychosocial tone* to consider. Behavioral scientists correctly contend there are motivators that leaders can infuse which will cause people to put forth more energy, effort, and enthusiasm into their work. Such "motivators" include: friendliness, recognition, praise, and appreciation. If a leader intentionally establishes and conveys a tone of acceptance, encouragement, empathy, forgiveness, support, and love while leading, others will be far more motivated to perform than if the opposite culture exists. A good example of this was Pat Summitt's personal guidelines in dealing with her athletes: honesty, compassion, generosity, and discipline.

People are motivated to perform at a higher level when interacting with leaders who genuinely care about them. Everyone needs to be appreciated and valued. Leadership consultant J.C. Hunter poignantly summarizes this truth: "I have learned that employees have a subconscious question the leader needs to answer on a regular basis – if not directly, then by his or her actions. That question is simply 'Are you glad I'm here?'" When people realize their leaders are interested in creating a relationship with them, they are often eager to "give back" or "work hard for their leader." Good leaders recognize their responsibility to proactively establish an engaging, caring climate within the organization.

**Value** is perhaps the most challenging and important variable in understanding and heightening a person's ability to be a self-starter. When an individual perceives value in a given task, they will be far more likely to contribute their maximum efforts toward achieving the objective.

One of the most disturbing tragedies in America today is the number of students who fail to complete their high school education. Statistics sadly reveal that 25% of students across the country do not graduate from high school. Indifference towards learning is rampant in too many classrooms, with students failing to study because they do not perceive relevant value in assignments. This is an example where leaders (teachers) must intensify efforts to clearly articulate to students what the advantage (value) is to students' personal lives to help them excel in required assignments. The most outstanding teachers will provide choices for students and make the curriculum and instruction particularly relevant to students' experiences, cultures, and long-term goals, enabling them to see value in the curriculum. Teachers can play a more direct role in motivating students by guiding them to see the lifelong benefits educational effort affords.

After surveying hundreds of American classrooms in the 1980s, education expert William Glasser discovered that today's students are apathetic because "there is not enough immediate payoff either in or out of school." Students did not perceive enough value for themselves personally to follow through on what was asked of them by their teachers. It is nearly impossible to motivate others if there is a sense that the work is not worthwhile. Glasser succinctly describes the ongoing challenge facing teachers: "If what is being taught does not satisfy the needs about which a student is currently most concerned, it will make little difference how brilliantly the teacher teaches – the student will not work to learn."

Throughout life, we are challenged to comprehend the inherent value of fulfilling many daily responsibilities. It is not natural to want to diet and exercise, pay taxes, drive the speed limit, tithe, or clean the house. It sure helps to set reasonable *expectations* in a positive *climate* and undertaking tasks with clearly understood *value* to our lives. Careful analysis of why we become motivated to do anything in life on a regular basis undoubtedly reveals an elevated level of each of these variables.

In Toyota factories around the world, employees pursue excellence in their work because they are literally shown the value of their work. The Toyota system empowers employees to think independently and take individual ownership. Instead of performing routine tasks without regard for their purpose, they are expected to contribute to the embedded culture of *Kaizen*. *Kaizen*, the relentless pursuit of continuous improvement, is credited for galvanizing performance among assembly line workers and in corporate offices, helping Toyota become the leading car manufacturer in the world.

A good leader is someone who has cultivated the ability to "cause positive change" within their family or organization. Leaders must consciously help others become lifelong *self-starters*. Many leaders shirk this critical responsibility by assuming it is up to their followers to motivate themselves. Former NBA star Swen Nater and UCLA professor Ron Galimore in their book titled – *You Haven't Taught Until They Have Learned,* assert that what leaders see in the attitudes and actions of their followers is either what has been *taught* or *permitted*. In this book the authors chronicle Coach John Wooden's teaching principles which helped him lead UCLA to ten NCAA National Basketball Championships. Wooden, the master teacher, coach, and motivator, embraced the opportunity to teach and inspire his players to become successful on and off the basketball court. Despite recruiting some of the finest athletes in America to his program he never assumed that they were naturally motivated and able to automatically succeed. He cherished his role as a teacher and motivator, making sure his teaching led to "learning" as reflected by his athletes' performances on the basketball court. Coach Wooden succinctly summarized the teacher's role in the education process as he posited: "No matter how cleverly I designed my lesson, or how smoothly it went, if the students didn't learn, I had not taught." Through taking such sincere responsibility for his students, he both unleashed the best within himself while he simultaneously brought out the best in others.

Successful leaders throughout history have been highly motivated individuals. Not that great leaders do not have to ward off days of apathy or indifference as motivation levels naturally wax and wane throughout life. The three essential variables of "expectation, climate, and value" must continually be reconciled and reinforced. The greater the value of each variable, the easier it will be to ignite self-starting behavior. The neglect of any one variable can diminish motivation and sadly lead to apathy and indifference. *Champions for Life* are motivated leaders who strive to maximize their talents to the fullest.

# "Champions are Motivated"
*Championship Points*

1. Motivation is an acquired trait, not a genetic gift.

2. Motivation is not dependent on environment, health, or wealth.

3. Motivated people are self-starters with strong values.

4. Motivation is contagious.

5. Motivated people are beacons to others.

6. Love is the most potent motivating force.

7. A genuine belief in others is central for a leader to motivate others.

8. Fear and incentives are temporary motivators.

9. Goal setting motivates and leads to excellence.

10. A strong relationship based on honesty, concern, and trust is the best motivation.

11. Motivation is enhanced with a clear purpose.

# Chapter 7
## "Champions are Courageous"

*"Courage is not the absence of fear, but rather the judgment that
something else is more important than fear."*

*(Ambrose Redmoon)*

"We're off to see the Wizard" sang Dorothy and her new friends strolling down the yellow brick road on their quest to see Oz. The strawman Scarecrow was desperate for a brain while his Tin Man companion yearned for a heart. The third of the eccentric trio, the Lion – the King of the Jungle - lived in shame because he was devoid of courage. The creators of this legendary masterpiece highlighted two essential organs of the body and the critical characteristic of courage. Perhaps they intuitively knew, in the words of Winston Churchill, that "Courage is the most important of all virtues because it guarantees the rest." Courage must be developed before anyone can ever become a championship human being, or in the lion's case, the "king of the jungle."

Courage is an acquired state of mind empowering a person to bravely face difficulties, dangers, or pain. Courageous people act when others stand frozen and sacrifice for causes perceived to be worthwhile and noble. Courage takes many forms. It can be of a physical nature needed to scale a mountain, block an All-State defensive end, or patrol the hostile terrain in enemy territory. Courage may also be morally rooted in an adolescent enabling him or her to withstand ridicule for doing what is right, a taxpayer to claim honest deductions on income tax forms, or a CEO to follow environmental guidelines even if extra costs are incurred. Courage is less the absence of fear than the willingness to do what is right regardless of the cost, and in spite of fears. Those who are admiringly hailed as intrepid have strapped on their fear and moved ahead anyway. Courage is a staple of greatness with ramifications that dare not be underestimated, as commitment to a great cause assailed by adversity is the breeding ground for heroism. President Reagan captured this concept: "We are the land of the free because we are the home of the brave."

Courage is an outcrop of strong character and belief in what is at stake. Consider 32 year-old Todd Beamer, who woke up one morning never suspecting his courage would soon be put to the ultimate test. On September 11, 2001, Todd boarded a plane in Newark, New Jersey for a routine business trip to San Francisco. Shortly after takeoff he and 37 other passengers quickly realized something was frighteningly awry as the plane reversed course. Beamer placed a call routed to a GTE customer-service representative who provided information about two planes hitting the Twin Towers. Todd realized what the wicked intentions of the terrorists were who now controlled the plane. He and three other passengers summoned their courage, deciding "they would not be pawns in the hijackers' suicidal plot." After praying the 23rd Psalm with the operator, Todd could be overheard exhorting "Are you guys ready? Let's roll," just before storming the cockpit to foil the terrorists' plans of crashing into the White House or U.S. Capitol. Todd's heroic action was guided by his steely character and fueled by the belief that thousands of innocent lives likely were at stake.

Gordon Brown, in his salient book titled *Courage,* describes the life of the German churchman Dietrich Bonhoeffer, who was executed for his resistance against the Nazis. Bonhoeffer, after deciphering the evil nature of the Nazi regime, stood in opposition to their cruel injustices even though he knew it would lead to certain death. Brown wrote that Bonhoeffer's life shows that "strength of belief is not enough: it needs to be matched by strength of character. Strong belief and weak character can all too easily amount to nothing more than moral cowardice." Bonhoeffer, like Todd Beamer, had both strong character and strong belief in what was right and needed at vital moments in history.

Courage is rooted in faith in the Lord. We know that Jesus' temperament was normally one of gentleness. Yet there are several occasions when His fortitude was vividly on display. He used a whip to drive the moneychangers, who were making a mockery of the Lord's House of Worship, out of the temple in Jerusalem, showing the resolve to take countercultural action for the sake of righteousness. More dramatically, voluntarily surrendering Himself to be savagely beaten, mocked, and murdered by crucifixion was the act of supreme courage and sacrifice. His courage to do what was right came from the depth of His relationship with His Father and His love and concern for the eternal welfare of human beings. John Maxwell writes: "His courage came from His sufficiency in His Father, which allowed Him to carry out unpopular tasks and leave His unforgettable mark."

Critical components of courage can also be found in a story about one of Jesus' disciples known historically as "Doubting Thomas." He earned that dubious moniker for questioning some of his fellow disciples' claims that Jesus had been raised from the dead, famously stating, "Unless I see, I will not believe." But Thomas, although he would be chided throughout the millennia for needing to see, also had a deep trust and faith in Jesus which produced a remarkable courage as revealed in the following story.

When Jesus and the disciples were near Judea, many of the religious leaders there were so offended by His claims and miracles they threatened to kill Him and His followers if they ever returned. So when word came to Jesus that His dear friend Lazarus was desperately ill, He waited a couple of days and then informed His disciples they were returning to Judea to see Lazarus. This unleashed a wave of fear among the 12 disciples convinced that they would surely be killed. As they were fretting, Jesus further shared that Lazarus was dead, but that they needed to go to him. The uneasy dread which now paralyzed the disciples with a sense of impending doom was finally shattered by Thomas, who boldly commanded, "Let us go, that we may die with Him." (John 11:16). Thomas would not abandon Jesus regardless of the potential cost, and because of it he and the other 11 were blessed beyond belief. By the time Jesus, Thomas, and the rest arrived in Bethany of Judea, Lazarus had already been in his tomb for four days. But Jesus, undaunted by this reality, commanded that the stone sealing Lazarus' grave be removed, and cried out in a loud voice, "Lazarus come forth!" Moments later, wrapped in burial cloth, Lazarus slowly shuffled out of the tomb free from the bonds of death. This is a seminal moment in history, a display of powerful hope beyond anyone's wildest imaginations - the return to life of a deceased mortal. Because Thomas had courage, the willingness to do right regardless of the cost, and well-placed faith, he and his friends witnessed the greatest miracle in human history. Thomas shows us that the best courage flows from an unbreakable love for others and trust in the Lord.

There is a natural ebb and flow to the level of courage in a person's heart dependent upon conviction and purpose. All people, like Dorothy's lion, naturally want to be brave and courageous, but experience times when paralyzing fear intrudes. Martin Luther King, Jr. is a prime example of someone who conquered doubts about his courage when he and his family were subjected to personal intimidation and violence during the boycott of the Montgomery bus system. King candidly describes the feelings he had sitting alone late one night at his kitchen table after receiving yet another call threatening to kill him and his family:

> With my cup of coffee sitting untouched before me, I tried to think of a way to move out of the picture without appearing a coward. I sat there and thought about a beautiful little daughter who had just been born. I'd come in night after night and see that little gentle smile. I started thinking about a dedicated and loyal wife, who was over there asleep. And she could be taken from me, or I could be taken from her. And I got to the point that I couldn't take it any longer. I was weak... The words I spoke to God that midnight are still vivid in my memory: 'Lord, I must confess that I'm weak now, I'm faltering. I'm losing my courage. Now, I am afraid.'

In his autobiography, King wrote that his courage was restored when he heard an inner voice prompting him to "Stand up for righteousness. Stand up for justice. Stand up for truth." As clarity of conviction and power of purpose crystalize, courage rises.

In the realm of athletics, one of the blessings of participating in sports such as football, basketball, wrestling, soccer, hockey, rugby, water polo, and others is the opportunity to develop physical courage. Coaches can create situations in drills designed to challenge and overcome the powerful instinct for self-preservation, replacing it with proactive toughness and ultimately self-sacrifice. Author John Eldridge writes: "A man must have a fight, a great mission... he must have a cause to which he is devoted... This is written into the fabric of his being." That is one of many reasons Jim has relished coaching football for almost 30 years. It gives boys the special fight referred to by Mr. Eldridge. s coaches, it is our responsibility to help them discover the hero within themselves. Each needs to become the hero in their own life story, whether it's as scout team running back or starting linebacker. There are no bit roles in preparing them to be *Champions for Life*. Each desperately wants and needs to know that he has got what it takes to be authentically courageous in his role. It is important for coaches when they see athletes demonstrate that courage to recognize and honor it. They will carry that affirmation from adults they respect for the rest of their lives. It becomes a rite of passage for a young man to know unequivocally that when his courage and toughness were put to the test, he did not succumb to fear. They are created from the image and likeness of God, the One who, when put to the ultimate test, came through for us because of His commitment and courage. This is one reason athletics is such a tremendous training ground for the tougher things in life yet to come, where the stakes will be raised even to the point of life and death.

The greatest expunger of fear is Jesus Christ because of His transformative power in our lives. Nothing, including our worst fears, can stand on solid ground in opposition to the Lord. Jim first learned this important truth his sophomore year in high school after a very difficult freshman year. During his first year in high school he discovered the awful reality of racial hatred and violence. He walked throughout his campus in a constant state of dread, fearing that he would be victimized by some who despised him for his skin tone. But things changed in the summer before his sophomore year and continued through the resumption of school. He deliberately sought a close relationship with the Lord. He read scripture and prayed frequently. The more God took priority in his life, the more his fear dissipated. That combined with a growing confidence gained from participation in challenging athletics in such a way he no longer swam in a sea of fear. Fear was instead replaced by a serene assurance that gave him a much greater ability to deal effectively with occasional extortionists and physical assaults. He came to comprehend what Jesus meant when he exhorted all of us: "Do not be afraid of those who kill the body but cannot kill the soul. Rather, be afraid of the One who can destroy both the body and the soul" (Matthew 10:28).

Anything that cannot affect us eternally is a "paper dragon." It may appear to be intimidatingly ominous, but it can do no permanent harm. A well-known acronym is constructed from F.E.A.R. – False Evidence Appearing Real. That is precisely what *paper dragons* in our lives are, looming over us menacingly, seeking to immobilize us while causing us to cower. Most of all they seek to drive a wedge of fear between us and God.  For Jim, once he surrendered to the Lord he understood where he'd come from; he knew God considered him to be part of His Family, that He had sacrificed everything for him. That is a powerful lineage to be a part of. Jim had faced trials in football and school that had enlarged his confidence. He saw that his toughest enemy that required defeat wasn't any gang member filled with hate, but his own fear. Unable to conquer it on his own, he sought Christ and found that His grace and strength were more than sufficient to free him from the dread that had held him hostage for a year.

Linking ourselves to the Creator, Redeemer, and Sustainer of our lives produces incredible benefits as we live in a tough world. The core truth of this is captivatingly and mesmerizingly conveyed near the end of the movie, *Amistad*. In a dramatic courtroom soliloquy, John Quincy Adams, portrayed brilliantly by Anthony Hopkins, delivers his closing argument trying to persuade the Supreme Court to free some Africans who had been unjustly enslaved and brutalized:

> When a member of the Mende Tribe in Africa encounters a desperate situation, he invokes his ancestors and tradition. You see, the Mende believe if they can summon the spirits of their ancestors, then they have never left, and the wisdom and strength they fathered and inspired will come to his aid… James Madison, Alexander Hamilton, Benjamin Franklin, Thomas Jefferson, George Washington, John Adams, we have long resisted asking you for guidance. Perhaps we have feared in doing so we might acknowledge that our own individuality, which we so revere, is not entirely our own. Perhaps we have feared an appeal to you might be taken for weakness. But we've come to understand now and embrace the understanding that who we are is who we were. We desperately need your strength and wisdom to triumph over our own fears, our prejudices, and ourselves. Give us the courage to do what is right.

At age 15, if Jim could have put into words what he was doing in seeking the Lord to help him in his desperation, he would have echoed the message and sentiments articulated so brilliantly by John Quincy Adams above. The Lord is the antidote for our worst fears and doubts. If it is true, as St. Paul writes in Ephesians 6:12, "Our struggle is not against flesh and blood, but against the rulers, against the authorities, against the powers of this dark world..." then we tremendously need support from the heavenly realm. But the Lord is there to meet that need. So often it is the last place we think of turning when it ought to be the first. The prophets, disciples, and apostles of ancient days, just like the Founding Fathers in the Amistad reference, are a timeless source of strength and inspiration in both word and deed, beautifully combining wisdom with courage.

Abraham Lincoln talked about the absolute necessity of courageous action when he wrote, "The war will not be won by strategy alone, but more by hard, fierce fighting." Lincoln understood there is no substitute for courage. The Navy SEALS are legendary for combining strategy, skill, and fanatical training. This includes instilling the virtue of courage and the benefits of taking courageous action or making a courageous stand. They understand that relentless physical resolve based on unity of purpose creates an unstoppable force. That is why their preparation is one of the most ruthlessly challenging of any fighting unit in the world.

Courage is also cultivated from setting high expectations. In the movie, *Invictus*, President Mandela invites the captain of the South African rugby team, a highly visible symbol of the previous Apartheid regime, to meet with him. He asks Francois Pinnear what his philosophy of leadership is, and how he infuses his men with courage. Francois answers the President, "By leading by example." Mr. Mandela concurs, but then adds that the real challenge for a leader is to get people to become better than they think they can be. He continues to ask, rhetorically, how do we inspire ourselves and others to greatness when nothing less will do? He explains we need to lean on the courageous accomplishments and greatness of others. During his darkest days of imprisonment, Mr. Mandela shares with Francois, he recalled the stanzas from a Victorian poem, "Invictus," which is Latin for "unconquerable." He concludes his homily by telling the rugby captain that to build a new and just nation, they must all exceed their own expectations. What is unstated but understood is that Francois and his teammates must set a standard which might seem impractical, but which will prove indispensable to success. As the poet Robert Browning mused, "A man's reach should exceed his grasp, or what's a heaven for." It is amazing the courage Francois and his teammates culled from raising the bar, ultimately winning the world championship and helping unite a nation on the verge of civil war.

When Martin Luther King Jr. proclaimed that he had seen the "promised land" and was not fearful of any man, it reflected such a passionate focus on justice and a hope for a better world that fear was literally banished from his heart and soul. Courage flows from a passionate purpose, whether it's a lineman wanting to protect his quarterback, a civil rights leader fulfilling his mission, or a Navy SEAL putting himself in the line of fire to save a fellow soldier. Andrew Jackson once proclaimed, "One leader with courage makes a majority," which is reinforced by the saying, "An army of deer led by a lion is more potent than an army of lions led by a deer." Tom Brokaw and many historians have referred to Americans who fought and won World War II as the "Greatest Generation." Why? Because the vast majority of soldiers were courageous "lions" committed to a righteous cause to the point of laying down their lives. They did it without fanfare or a desire for acclamation, but rather for a purpose worthy of complete commitment.

Revolutionary troops followed George Washington largely because he was the embodiment of courage. When they would engage the British, he was often on the front lines facing the first bullets while leading the charge. When Mel Gibson, portraying William Wallace in *Braveheart*, said that men don't follow titles, they follow courage, he was describing a future General Washington and Colonel Chamberlain.

Colonel Joshua Lawrence Chamberlain's heroism and bravery at Little Round Top during the Battle of Gettysburg continues to shape history almost 160 years later. In early July 1863, General Robert E. Lee's substantial rebel force was poised to outflank and overrun Union forces near a small southern Pennsylvania town. With a victory at Gettysburg, the Confederacy would probably have won the Civil War. America may have fragmented into several countries over time. Slavery likely would have continued with all its attendant atrocities and suffering. There would have been no United States of America to come to Europe's defense in World War I or Europe's and Asia's defense in World War II.

But the extreme flank of the Union army was not overrun because of the leadership and supreme courage of a 34-year-old professor from Maine. He led a regiment that had lost 70% of its men in two years of bloody fighting prior to Gettysburg. And now here he was with the remaining 300, with strict orders to not surrender or retreat because of the strategic value of the spot he was assigned to hold at all costs. As rebel forces continued to batter his depleted, bloodied, and exhausted regiment, Colonel Chamberlain's men started to run out of ammunition. Late in the afternoon on this hot, humid July day, southern regiments from Alabama and Texas prepared for a final overwhelming uphill assault against the 80 men left under Colonel Chamberlain's command. When they began their attack, the Professor realized they would have no chance if they simply tried to hold the high ground. Surrender was not an option and he wasn't about to see his men shot in the back running away. He had shared with his men prior to this climactic crucible the pivotal nature of the looming battle, one that could cause the permanent enslavement of many of their fellow countrymen. Now facing almost certain death and defeat against a superior force, but fueled by a passionate purpose, Colonel Chamberlain leapt up on a rock, yelled for his men to fix bayonets and ordered a charge. The courageous maneuver shocked and fragmented the advancing Rebels who assumed these Yankees were part of a larger reinforcement, and the gray clad troops fled in the face of Chamberlain's onslaught. One man's courage and leadership saved the Union army on that fateful day, and ultimately General Lee retreated back into Virginia instead of marching unopposed into Washington.

In another riveting scene from the epic movie *Gladiator*, the hero Maximus is confronted by the evil emperor, Commodus, in the Coliseum:

Commodus: "Slave! You will remove your helmet and tell me your name!"

Maximus: My name is Maximus Decimus Meridias, Commander of the armies of the north, General of the Felix Legions, loyal servant to the true emperor, Marcus Aurelius; father to a murdered son, husband to a murdered wife, and I will have my vengeance, in this life or the next!"

Commenting on this poignant scene in his book *Wild at Heart*, John Eldridge writes: "Maximus' answer builds like a wave, swelling in size and strength before crashing on shore. Where does a man go to learn an answer like that - to learn his true name… which can never be taken from him? You have to know where you've come from; you have to have faced a series of trials that test you… you have to have faced your enemy." When confronted by our worst fears and doubts, how do we stand tall?

Fear is a pervasive challenge a leader must help his charges defeat. Identifying our fears, our *real opposition*, and courageously subduing them is a prerequisite to becoming a championship human being.  Just as teams in any sport have opponents they will try to triumph over, so too do individuals have a daunting set of obstacles that must be identified and overcome. Chinese strategist Sun Tzu in his classic *The Art of War* reminds us it is not enough to know ourselves well; we also must know and understand our enemies. Seasoned coaches or executives who lead teams or organizations recognize that the opponents or competition are neither the toughest nor most hazardous impediments to be faced. Instead, those opponents merely become the tests to courageously prepare for and then see how much an organization has learned, grown, and overcome.

Beacons of courage like Colonel Chamberlain, Dr. King, and President Mandela are critical because a society writes its diary by naming its heroes. These men, with others like Reverend Billy Graham, Pope John Paul II, and Russian writer Aleksandr Solzhenitsyn, blended a vision for a better world for the people they served with the embodiment of truth, justice, empathy, and forgiveness. Many lived under constant threat of death, and yet were armed with only truth and justice. They could do this in part because of what Solzhenitsyn articulated: "One word of truth outweighs the whole world." They stand in sharp contrast with our present shallow society, obsessed with celebrities who crave attention and adulation. Heroes instead desire to make a big difference – not to receive, but to give. They live with a deep commitment to courageously do what is right combined with a selfless love for those God places in their path. Heroes are all about service and sacrifice, and in that process they shape our values, build our character through example, and clarify what is important.

Many iconic leaders have had virtuous traits embossed on their hearts from their earliest youth, and when put to the extreme test, their courage rose in unstoppable waves. Miguel de Cervantes asserts: "He who loses wealth, loses much. He who loses a friend, loses more. He who loses courage, loses all." Courageous leaders throughout history recognize that all could be lost and have instead galvanized small groups of often fatigued and frightened individuals to take heroic steps to save their country and their dream of freedom. Courage is often the most influential characteristic necessary for *Champions for Life* to forge a path that leads to victory.

# "Champions are Courageous"
*Championship Points*

1. Courage is not an absence of fear.

2. Courage is the willingness to do what is right.

3. Observing courage in action is never forgotten.

4. People admire and follow the courageous.

5. Courage is the pathway to greatness.

6. Courage is cultivated from high expectations and a passionate purpose.

7. Great feats always begin with courage.

8. Acts of courage have eternal significance.

9. History admires the wise, but places the courageous on a pedestal.

# Chapter 8
## "Champions are Determined"

*"Never give in. Never give in. Never, never, never, never--in nothing, great or small, large or petty--never give in, except to convictions of honor and good sense. Never yield to force. Never yield to the apparently overwhelming might of the enemy."*

*(Winston Churchill – 1941)*

A key characteristic found in successful people is determination. Determination is the conviction to never give up. A familiar adage in American lore is "if at first you don't succeed, try, try again." Sadly, the motto that seems to prevail in society today is "if at first you don't succeed, try something else – or someone else." It has become commonplace for people to begin something today and give up tomorrow after quickly succumbing to adversity or unpleasant obstacles. It takes no talent to try something and quit. Conversely, it takes a special person to relentlessly persevere through daunting obstacles in life to reach a worthy goal.

Examples of people who navigate through life with unwavering determination are becoming increasingly rare. However, there are inspirational stories of determined people that serve as poignant reminders of what is possible when this essential value has been instilled in a true *champion's* character. Consider the biography of Abraham Lincoln whose determination is chronicled by the following events:

| | |
|---|---|
| 1831 | Failed in business |
| 1832 | Defeated for the Legislature |
| 1833 | Again failed in business |
| 1834 | Elected to the Legislature |
| 1835 | Sweetheart died |
| 1836 | Had a nervous breakdown |
| 1838 | Defeated for Speaker |
| 1840 | Defeated for Elector |
| 1843 | Defeated for Congress |

|      |                                     |
|------|-------------------------------------|
| 1846 | Elected to Congress                 |
| 1848 | Defeated for Congress               |
| 1855 | Defeated for Senate                 |
| 1856 | Defeated for Vice-President         |
| 1858 | Defeated for Senate                 |
| 1860 | Elected PRESIDENT OF THE UNITED STATES |

Wow! It defied logic for Lincoln to continue his quest of becoming a political leader, but his resolve to follow his convictions led him to become one of the most inspirational and influential people in history. Thankfully, Abraham Lincoln was not detoured by his embarrassing defeats from pursuing his goal to eradicate slavery and preserve the union. Surely Theodore Roosevelt must have had President Lincoln in mind when he penned: "The credit belongs to the man who is actually in the arena, whose face is marred with sweat and dust and blood, who spends himself in a worthy cause, and if he fails, at least fails while daring greatly so that his place shall never be with those cold and timid souls who know neither victory nor defeat."

In his book titled *Success is Overrated* – Geoff Colvin describes how it is tempting to look at successful individuals and naturally conclude they have been given an extra dose of genetic favor. However, Colvin exposes this myth by proving the key ingredients in success are determination and hard work. There is absolutely no evidence of a "fast track" for high achievers. Colvin asserts that the "factor that seems to explain the most about great performance is deliberate practice... Deliberate practice is hard. It hurts. But it works. More of it equals better performance. Tons of it equals great performance." This determined work ethic is epitomized in Olympic hero Michael Phelps, winner of eight gold medals in the 2008 Olympics, who reported swimming every day for five straight years before diving into the pool in Beijing. A determined lifestyle is the norm for millions of Chinese rice farmers who rise before dawn 365 days a year to carefully sculpt and tend their small rice paddies in suffocating heat and humidity to produce life-sustaining food. Great feats in life, whether in the pool, muddy fields, science labs, or anywhere else always include a visceral dose of determination.

There is nothing more common in life than to see potentially successful "rice farmers" raise the proverbial white flag when facing the first bad rain. Countless athletes, students, salespeople, or aspiring leaders who had more than enough talent to reach great heights, gave up too early after their first losing season, poor report card, cold call rejection, or subpar board review. The resolve to fight through discouraging setbacks, embarrassment, and pain is not a genetic gift, but a conscious decision made on a daily or sometimes hourly basis.

Winston Churchill had the reputation of a bulldog because of his determination to fight through unimaginable adversity during World War II. An inspiring example of this determination is found in the following story about a real bulldog. This stumpy animal is not necessarily a prize to look at, but is a prime example of a relentless creature. The story is told that there was once a pastor who owned two prized hunting dogs. These two sleek beauties played in his backyard daily. One day, however, down the alley came a cantankerous bulldog that saw the hunting dogs in the backyard and crawled through a small hole under the fence to challenge them. The hunting dogs looked at the bulldog, and the pastor looked at his hunting dogs. The pastor thought to himself that he would let the bulldog learn valuable lesson about his obvious limitations while letting nature take its course. Sure enough the hunting dogs attacked the bulldog. The bulldog after rolling around on the ground whimpering ad injured, scampered back through the hole in the fence and limped back home down the alley. The pastor and the hunting dogs thought that that was the end of the bulldog. Shortly after that, the pastor left town for a few days to attend a conference. When he returned, his wife told him to come to the backyard at once. The prized hunting dogs were in the backyard playing as usual when the same bulldog came down the alley. Sure enough, the bulldog crawled through the hole in the fence and suddenly, the prized hunting dogs ran as fast as they could towards the doggie door and were found shaking downstairs in the basement. Meanwhile, the bulldog could be seen strutting around the backyard before helping himself to the hunting dogs' food. The pastor was incredulous and asked his wife what had happened while he was out of town. The pastor's wife replied, "Honey, *every day* while you were gone, the bulldog came back and took his whipping by your prized hunting dogs, and just yesterday, your prized hunting dogs had had enough." This story captures the essential precursor to success. Did you catch it? EVERY DAY the bulldog came back, even when it made no sense for him to do so. Talk about determination!

History reveals determined individuals who became inspirational beacons for millions. Charles Lindbergh never gave up on his quest to become the first solo aviator to successfully fly 3,600 miles nonstop across the Atlantic by achieving that feat in 33 ½ hours in 1927. This milestone was achieved only after overcoming setback after setback for many years. Lou Gehrig, played in 2,130 consecutive games despite suffering from 17 different fractured bones while continuing to play until acquiring a terminal illness, which ended his life at the age of 37. The "Iron Horse" earned his nickname! Ben Hogan was nearly killed in a car accident that crushed his legs, causing him to struggle to even walk for the rest of his life. But 16 months after his near fatal crash, he won the U.S. Open Golf Championship, and ultimately five more major championships. While suffering from diabetes at the age of 52, Ray Croc had his gallbladder and most of his thyroid gland surgically removed. Instead of retreating from life, he opened a hamburger restaurant called McDonald's. Leaders of the Apollo space program did not scrap the vision to send a man to the moon after that tragic fire in the Apollo 1 training exercise on January 27, 1967, killed three brave astronauts. Two years later as Neil Armstrong set foot on the moon, he uttered the now-famous words, "That's one small step for a man, one giant leap for mankind." Giant leaps result from dogged determination. Legendary UCLA basketball coach John Wooden led the Bruins for 15 seasons before winning his first NCAA championship. Thankfully Coach Wooden did not give up nor did the administration give up on him before his first championship, which primed the pump to win a record total of ten, an unmatched feat. Superstar basketball player Michael Jordan was cut from his sophomore high school basketball team, sorely testing his pride and sense of determination. Fortunately for sports fans "Air Jordan" did not succumb to the temptation to quit, but instead, persevered and developed the skills to thrill millions of sports fans around the world while rewriting NBA history books. Young surfing phenomenon, Bethany Hamilton, inspired many by showing great resolve in continuing to win surfing championships after having an arm bitten off in a vicious shark attack while training in the waters off Hawaii. All of these extraordinary individuals demonstrate unfailingly that it is not what *happens* to you – it is how you *respond*. Success begins with a *decision* to be determined no matter what life throws at you.

The problem with giving up is that you never experience the great fortune that lies around the next corner in life. Ronald Reagan loved to tell the story of a little boy who was questioned why he was digging so furiously into a large pile of manure. His answer was simple, "there's got to be a pony in here!" How many great feats have gone unrealized because someone caved in to temporary adversity or fear? One of the most compelling examples of this occurs each winter during Midwestern snowstorms when drivers pull to the side of the road to wait for better conditions. Tragically, these people are often later found dead in their cars because they ran out of gas and froze to death, or asphyxiated themselves with carbon monoxide poisoning. These sad deaths are compounded when their cars are discovered only a short distance away from a gas station, hotel, or farm house. On a happier note, couples celebrating golden wedding anniversaries recount times in their marriages when they almost gave up and divorced only to persevere and come to realize a much deeper love for one another. You can only speculate on how many divorces could have been prevented with just one more day of counseling or one more candle-lit dinner. Or how many college scholarships could have been earned or championships won with one more hour a day of practice or study.

Sir Ernest Shackleton, the famous pioneer of Antarctica exploration, suffered his greatest failure between 1914-1916 when he lost his ship *Endurance* before ever reaching Antarctica. However, in this foiled expedition, Shackleton demonstrated great courage and determination as he saved the lives of the 22 men stranded with him for two years. Shackleton persevered against the harshest of physical conditions by embracing his personal mantra: "In trouble, danger, and disappointment never give up hope. The worst can always be got over." Because of Shackleton's heroism and wise guidance in the face of great peril, he has been hailed as one of the world's best leaders in history. Shackleton, who embraced his responsibility as a leader, summarized the essence of good leadership when he said: "If you're a leader, a fellow that other fellows look to, you've got to keep going."

While we as coaches and teachers have never had to navigate a ship through the icebergs of the Antarctic or fly a small prop plane solo over the Atlantic, we have endured challenging seasons and worked with students who failed on tests or projects. When failure hits, it hurts – particularly when scores are posted in the newspapers. When Kent accepted the offer to coach women's basketball at Concordia University Irvine, it was rather late in the spring. As a result he did not get to recruit any new players as scholarship commitments had already been solidified by his predecessor. The first year of his college coaching career saw the Eagles finish with 7 wins and 22 losses. As disappointing a year as that was, he grew optimistic for the second season because he could invest significant time and energy into recruiting new talent. Unfortunately, adversity struck the day before school began when his starting center, projected to be an All-American, withdrew from school for personal reasons. While it may not have been comparable to Shackleton's ordeal, he knows what it was like to finish with a 4-23 record. Some have said that "Gold is refined by fire." Well, Kent knows what it feels like to be in the fire. He also knows that determination is a learned value acquired from parents, teachers, coaches, pastors, and mentors. From these special people throughout his formative years, Kent had learned that quitting was repugnant and was thankful to a supportive administration to which "firing" was not an option. There are many reasons over the next three seasons he and the Eagles had a record of 72-18 and two trips to the NAIA National Tournament, but the essential component was a substantial dose of "determination" by singed proud athletes and coaches.

In the seminal study of what produces lasting excellence in companies, *Good to Great* author Jim Collins shares a noteworthy concept he describes as the Stockdale Paradox. It was based on the experiences of American POWs during the Vietnam War. It is named for Admiral James Stockdale, who was the highest ranking U.S. military officer incarcerated in the infamous Hanoi Hilton from 1965-1973, where he was tortured over 20 times. He had no rights, no release date, and no guarantee of survival. Asked how he could retain any optimism, Admiral Stockdale said he never lost faith in the end of the story. "I never doubted that not only would I get out, but also that I would prevail and turn the experience into the defining event in my life, which in retrospect, I would not trade." He was also asked who didn't make it out and why. "Oh, that's easy, the blind optimists. They were the ones who said, we'll be out by Christmas, and then Christmas would come and go. Then they would say Easter and same problem. They ended up dying of broken hearts…You must never confuse faith that you will prevail in the end with the discipline to confront the most brutal facts of reality." That is an exact description of what determined people do. They confront the most vexing realities of their current situation, but never lose sight or hope that victory will ultimately be theirs.

In football, Jim likes to remind his coaches to maintain a very determined, optimistic outlook by occasionally reassuring them before a game that those who truly love and care about them prior to kickoff will also love and care about them after the game. There is no critical relationship at stake. Therefore, he will encourage them to cut loose by leading with a poised, assertive mindset. This allows us to focus on helping the players by letting them see the belief we have in them in our eyes. As coaches, the games and their attendant spotlight are not about us as coaches. They're about them (the players) and the Lord, which frees us up to let go of ourselves and be the leaders they need. Jim will also remind the players of this truth, trying to help them focus on the play at hand, while not worrying about the scoreboard outcome.

UCLA football coach Chip Kelly's mantra has always been "Win the Day." Win the drill. Win the battle not to give into fatigue. Don't get carried away with dwelling on the future. This point is also driven into Navy SEALS during their toughest training crucible: Hell Week. Wise officers advise these special future warriors not to think even a day down the road, a thought process which can evoke a sense of overwhelming dread causing them to capitulate right when they're on the cusp of finishing their gauntlet. Determined athletes and warriors develop the capacity to energize their thoughts and galvanize their efforts on winning the moment or battle at hand. Scripture says it this way: "Do not worry about tomorrow, for tomorrow will worry about itself. Each day has enough trouble of its own" (Matthew 6:34).

As we navigate through life we will inevitably face times of adversity and suffering that arise because of our sin-soaked world. These twin adversaries can wound and weaken even the most principled individual. When a person experiences loss, sickness, pain, and tragedy it affects everything, eroding confidence and often assailing a person's faith in God. Adversity does, however, have its boundaries for all who believe in Jesus Christ. The following story of a wise Chinese farmer reflects this:

There was once a Chinese farmer who had one son and one horse. One day the farmer's one horse found an opening in the walls of the corral and ran away. The farmer's neighbors all came to him and said: "Oh, what bad luck." The farmer replied to his neighbors: "How do you know it is bad luck?" Later that same day the one horse returned to the farm with seven other wild horses seeking refuge. The farmer's neighbors ran to the farmer and said: "Oh, what good luck!" The farmer replied to his neighbors: "How do you know it is good luck?" Sure enough, later on when the farmer's one son was trying to train one of the new horses he was thrown to the ground and broke his leg. The farmer's neighbors came to the farmer and lamented: "Oh, what bad luck!" The farmer again replied to his neighbors: "How do you know it is bad luck?" Several weeks later Chinese warlords came to the village, conscripting all the strong able-bodied young men, forcing them off to war and passed on the injured son. The young men from the village were all killed in war, never to return to their homes.

The Chinese farmer's example teaches that adversity and fortune are relative. Events can be perceived as being very bad or very good but only time can ultimately reveal the true and enduring nature of events. The key to life is, like the Chinese farmer teaches us, to keep our eyes on the big picture. Adversity is often used by God to instruct us, protect us, prepare us, or strengthen us for a purpose or circumstance we do not yet perceive. Paul, the apostle of Christ who endured great hardships, reminds us in Romans 8:28 that "in all things God works for the good of those who love him, who have been called according to his purpose."

A major obstacle impeding us from experiencing abundant living is the temptation to blame others or difficult circumstances for our deficiencies or negative outcomes. Winners take responsibility for their actions and destiny. Whenever we point the finger at someone for our own mistakes or losses, it is a sign of our fallen sinful nature. We first witnessed this overt displacement of blame when Adam shamefully pointed the finger at his wife Eve for her poor advice. Eve immediately followed suit, quickly blaming the devil for causing her to pluck the forbidden fruit in the Garden of Eden. Not only was God dismayed by their lack of personal responsibility, but people today also are unimpressed by those who seek to absolve themselves from accountability. Famed journalist Edward R. Murrow once wisely noted: "Difficulty is the excuse history never accepts." No one is interested in excuses. No one is inspired or enriched by being blamed. From a leadership standpoint, the tendency to blame becomes a toxic habit difficult and slow to purge from our system. It is common, especially in athletics, for coaches and players to blame others for poor performance or less than stellar outcomes. Blaming in effect doubles the toxicity that should never have been allowed a foothold in the first place, and can instead directly lead to further unnecessary losses. There is a wise adage among good leaders: "Never allow one loss to beat you twice." This is avoided when we abstain from the sinful tendency to blame others for setbacks. Instead, each organizational member should accept responsibility for what improvements they can make in the wake of the lessons learned from defeat.

The inspiring story of Chris Gardner, portrayed so empathetically by Will Smith in the movie *The Pursuit of Happyness*, movingly demonstrates the power of the virtue of taking responsibility. Chris' world is rocked by financial misfortune and poor choices, and family disintegration which leave him and his toddler son homeless. Years later after he had climbed out of the pit of poverty and despair rising to tremendous financial and family success, he was asked during a national television interview what was the key to his turnaround. Without hesitation he responded, taking personal responsibility, refusing to blame circumstances or others for his lot in life. "In those days of living in a public restroom with my son, I had to ask myself some hard questions and face a tough reality. I recognized that I 'drove my own car' to this destination [the public bathroom]. If that were true, then it followed that I could drive out of there to a better place." He advised those experiencing personal difficulty to stop the excuse and blame game, which only paralyzes us, freezing us from taking proactive steps to better our circumstances and relationships.

In coaching, failure is both inevitable and public. But it doesn't become poisonous until it transitions from an event to a characteristic. While coaching football at Orange Lutheran High School Jim's mantra was: A person isn't a failure until he/she quits, blames others, makes excuses, or gives less than their best. Quitting implies the breaking of a commitment, and can occur on something as simple as a homework assignment or not finishing a block or rebound. Blame is insidious and, like selfishness, can shatter an organization's esprit de corps rapidly.

The only time a finger should be pointed is to pass along a compliment. Making excuses is the hallmark of failure. Ben Franklin once remarked that he "never knew a man good at making excuses who was good at anything else." How many times will you hear a coach before a season has even begun bemoan the youthfulness or inexperience of his or her squad. Some failure becomes prophetically assured with the planting of the excuse seeds. Finally, the secret to no regrets is giving our best!

One of the biggest challenges of living is no one can escape having to face adversity. Consider the example of Job, a very good man who endured the trauma of losing his entire family, fortune, and health just when he was experiencing great success and happiness. We learn through this timeless saga that adversity plays no favorites as Job was a man who "worshipped God and was faithful to Him. He was a good man, careful not to do anything evil." In Job 1:8 God himself describes Job: "There is no one on earth like him; he is blameless and upright, a man who fears God and shuns evil." Wow! No one on earth as good! Yet, Job's world turned upside down for an extended period of time when, literally, all hell broke loose.

The life of Job teaches us three valuable lessons. First, it is important for all of us to hold everything loosely in life. Our jobs, titles, wealth, homes, marriages, and health can all be taken from us even when we are doing everything right. This was certainly Job's case when he lost it all. Concentration camp survivor Corrie ten Boom puts it this way: "Hold everything in your hands lightly; otherwise it hurts when God pries your fingers open." Life, like championship seasons and organizations, is very fragile. A back injury to a starting point guard can decimate a team's playoff chances... a sudden division of skin cells can change a mole's status from benign to malignant... a dry summer and a deranged arsonist's spark can cause a raging inferno... an exciting employment promotion can seduce a loyal spouse into an affair... We need to be extremely thankful for every breath we breathe and every blessing because life is tenuous.

Second, Job teaches us we have one of two choices when staring into the teeth of adversity. We can become intensely disillusioned and embittered or embrace challenges as a platform on which to put our hope and trust in God. Job has served as a hero of the faith and template for millions over the centuries because of his demonstrated resolve to love and trust God despite his adversity. In Job 1:21-22, we get a glimpse of Job's attitude towards adversity: "Naked I came from my mother's womb, and naked I will depart. The Lord gave and the Lord has taken away; may the name of the Lord be praised... In all this, Job did not sin by charging God with wrongdoing."

We cannot help but be inspired when we see people swimming strongly against misfortune's tide, all the while displaying a positive attitude, determination, and sense of peace even as they struggle. Joni Erickson paints pictures today with a brush in her teeth while also speaking all over the world to large audiences about the joy in her life despite becoming a quadriplegic from a diving accident. Jim Abbott was born without a right hand and taught himself to pitch a baseball so well that he was able to win an Olympic gold medal and the Sullivan Award for being the best amateur athlete in America before playing 10 seasons of Major League Baseball. Tom Dempsey was born with half a right foot and no right hand but set the NFL field goal record of 63 yards in 1970, a record which stood until Matt Prater of the Denver Broncos bested it by one yard in 2013. These remarkable paragons encapsulate the empowering and encouraging words we find in James 1:2-3: "Consider it pure joy, my brothers, whenever you face trials of many kinds, because you know that the testing of your faith develops perseverance."

Finally, the life of Job teaches us that adversity has an end. The storms that rocked Job's life abated. The Lord once again blessed Job with family and fortune which he enjoyed for 140 years after his trials. During moments of agony and seeming hopelessness, Job clung to the strength and promises of God. Job knew that alone he was nothing, but that by God's grace he would eventually pass through even the valley of the shadow of death. Fortunately we too can acquire this same perspective and peace. Consider the deep insight shared by beloved Concordia University Irvine administrator Dr. Robert Baden shortly before his death from cancer: "The secret to facing the future is not to look ahead where we cannot see, but to look back at the Lord's blessings in the past, where we are reminded of His love and faithfulness." Job, along with Joni Erickson, Jim Abbott, and Tom Dempsey, in surveying their own lives, were reminded that the fires of adversity are never out of control in the hands of a loving God.

There is a fine line between success and failure in life. Championship seasons are so very fragile. When adversity strikes, *Champions* keep fighting. Dr. Randy Pausch, a brilliant professor of computer science at Carnegie Mellon University, became famous for delivering what came to be called 'The Last Lecture' before pancreatic cancer took his life at the age of 47. He urged others to understand that "The brick walls are there for a reason. The brick walls are not there to keep us out. The brick walls are there to give us a chance to show how badly we want something." Don't give up! Determination is an essential characteristic for great performances and one that leads *Champions for Life* to achieve ultimate success in every area of life.

# "Champions are Determined"
### *Championship Points*

1. There are no shortcuts to success; only determined efforts will get you there.

2. The best way to overcome adversity is to persist.

3. Determination is a conscious decision rather than random behavior.

4. Determination is a core component found in all greatness.

5. Determination and perspiration are potent allies.

6. Determination reflects uncommon commitment.

7. Determined people never lose sight of their goal.

8. Determination reveals the depth of our desire.

# Chapter 9
"Champions Can Communicate"

*"Communication works for those who work at it."*
(John Powell)

In Thomas Friedman's fascinating book, *The World is Flat,* he describes a world shrinking due to the explosion of technology services provided through the internet. This global metamorphosis has ushered in a new age where a tax return submitted from Irvine, California is processed and completed by accountants in Jaipur, India and MRI films generated in Wichita, Kansas can be analyzed by doctors in Melbourne, Australia. A byproduct of the disappearance of traditional economic borders and the consequent increased outsourcing of jobs has intensified competition for employment here in America. Friedman asserts those who wish to compete effectively in the 21$^{st}$ century must develop strong communication skills. Without honed communication capabilities individuals will face daunting personal marketability barriers which translate into substantial challenges to becoming a person of influence. Exacerbating this new climate is the fact that corporate recruiters regularly lament the lack of proficient writing and speaking skills among neophyte job seekers fresh out of college. The good news is, however, like so many components essential to become a *Champion for Life*, outstanding communication skills are not inherited genetically but can be acquired through diligent effort and concerted practice.

Poor communication is ominously pervasive in contemporary society. As George Bernard Shaw wryly noted, "The single biggest problem in communication is the illusion that it has taken place." Many of these problems can be traced to the simple inability of people to share ideas cogently. According to communications expert Patricia Buhler, miscommunication most often results from two basic, but faulty assumptions. "First, people tend to assume that they know what others mean. Second, people assume that others know what they mean." Minus effective oral and written skills, even the most highly educated professionals will quickly hit the inevitable "glass ceilings" on their career paths. The following study conducted at Purdue University by Robert Half bears this out:

> Purdue's engineering graduates were as well educated as graduates from other fine universities, but Purdue found that its graduates hadn't climbed as high or as fast on the corporate ladder as had other schools' graduates. Seeking a reason, the school compared its curriculum with those of the other schools. The answer was clear: Although all the core engineering curricula were similar, the other universities required many more courses in oral and written communication. Purdue revamped its curriculum, adding communications courses, and saw significant improvements in the career progression of its engineering graduates.

Sometimes poor communication is a symptom of a leader's lack of clarity about what she or he actually thinks and wishes to communicate. An essential prerequisite to communication is to be clear about what it is you are trying to convey. Half developed ideas, inconsistent thoughts, or incomplete concepts, will undermine communication even before you begin. Only once it is clear in your own mind what is to be communicated can you put to use the keys to good communication. Clarity comes before words.

Proficient communication is a composite of four identifiable components. These elements require careful cultivation and polishing before anyone can be a master communicator. The best communicators combine a command of the following four skills to produce communicative excellence.

1. **Nonverbal** - Dr. Buhler asserts that when people communicate, 60% of the message comes from body language, 30% from voice tone, and 10% from actual words spoken. Fredric H. Jones, a respected mentor for teachers contends that good classroom management is 95% nonverbal. When you carefully observe an effective teacher, coach, or parent you intuit the power inherent in nonverbal skills. Research suggests that a person has a mere seven seconds to make a positive first impression. Those initial

impressions are formed before a word is ever spoken. When you consider that none of us ever gets a second chance to make a good first impression, there is no substitute for getting it right the first time!

The initial message received when meeting someone or observing someone lead is visual in nature. This is true both in listening and in speaking. When one person makes eye contact with another, they communicate that they are *listening* to what is being said. This is a strong indicator of *respect* being given to the speaker. Maintaining eye contact with another person also communicates a sense of *honesty*. It is very difficult to lie to someone while looking them straight in the eye. People also sense a high level of *confidence* in the person who can look them square in the eye when talking. Champions embrace the power of eye contact as they know it communicates they are listening respectfully to other people, they are honest in what they are saying, and have confidence in themselves. In our athletic programs and classrooms, we emphasized listening with our eyes and our ears.

The second nonverbal skill that communicates volumes is body posture. It is wise to remember the power of standing whenever anyone approaches to greet you or shake your hand. This simple act of respect can leave a lasting positive impression. Both of us had the pleasure of meeting one of America's most revered football coaches, the University of Nebraska's Dr. Tom Osborne, just minutes prior to his address to a large audience at the American Football Coaches Association Convention in Anaheim, California. Neither of us will forget how he stood from his chair, turned towards us, and made warm and sincere eye contact as he shook our hands while engaging in polite introductions. Coach Osborne understands the maxim there is no second chance to make a good first impression. Consequently he never forfeits the invaluable opportunity to communicate positively regardless if the person is a well-known dignitary or complete strangers as we were. Champions never underestimate the power of their eyes and body posture.

So many children or employees have experienced the deflating effects of nonverbal communication because a parent puts their head in their hands after a missed layup or strike out, or a boss reflects disinterest with crossed arms or fleeting focus while listening to a presentation that took weeks to prepare, or even the crushing blow a spouse can deliver unintentionally with a simple frown after a painstakingly beautiful dinner has been prepared. The stakes can also be immeasurably higher. During a 1992 Presidential Debate, George H.W. Bush made a costly gaffe prior to responding to a question about how the deep recession had personally affected him. Instead of maintaining eye contact with the panelist, he stole a quick look at his wristwatch, conveying a disinterest or unease with a topic of paramount visceral concern to the American public. History Professor Ellen Fitzpatrick of the University of New Hampshire insightfully commented that the President's seemingly innocuous glance "became freighted with deeper meaning."

The third nonverbal skill originated as an international custom centuries ago to show that a person came in peace without weaponry. The handshake is a powerful purveyor of openness, enthusiasm, acceptance, confidence, forgiveness, and simple friendliness. Indira Gandhi wisely noted that "you cannot shake hands with a fist." As head basketball coach at Concordia University, Kent created a "Handshake Rule" during his second coaching season there. He was concerned about the prospects for declining team morale as the season wore on given the low level of squad success. As the preseason began, Kent insisted that every time anyone in the Lady Eagle basketball program saw each other they were to shake hands. The penalty for failing to greet one another properly was a mile run for the team. He fretted initially that the newly embraced practice of shaking each other's hand was due merely to fear of the penalty. However, he quickly learned that the new behavior had become contagious because of the genuinely positive feelings a friendly outstretched hand was evoking. Soon no one even remembered the punishment aspect because the young women enjoyed the new friendship ritual so much.

In January of 2011, we had the privilege of attending the University of Tennessee's Lady Vols basketball practice and meeting and observing legendary Head Coach Pat Summitt. The all-time winningest basketball coach at that time among men or women, was the consummate "court General" exuding confidence and competence. It was very clear to us as observers that her commanding presence set the tone for an exceptional practice before the players even commenced their first drill. Her nonverbal interactions with each assistant coach and player conveyed a depth of caring while simultaneously prompting effort worthy of one of the elite teams in the country. All without ever saying a word!

Champions are adept at taking advantage of the opportunity to communicate a positive message through nonverbal skills. What we *do* in life is usually remembered so much longer than what we *say*. People would rather *see* a sermon than *hear* one any day. There really is power to change lives in messages sent without ever speaking a word. As St. Francis sagely advised, "Preach the Gospel at all times and if necessary use words."

2. *Verbal* - The mouth can't stay closed forever. Champions must learn to speak and clearly articulate their ideas. Although public speaking is one of most peoples' greatest fears, it is reassuring to know that well known speakers and performers such as Billy Graham, John F. Kennedy, Barbra Streisand, and Sir Laurence Olivier admitted having to overcome fear of being in front of large groups early in their careers. During the 1960 presidential campaign, Jim's father attended a large rally for JFK. In an overflow crowd he stood directly to the side of the future president about 30 yards away. Despite the distance, he could see Senator Kennedy's hands shaking with nervousness even while his voice was one of clear conviction and confidence. Mark Twain said it best, "There are two types of speakers: those that are nervous and those that are liars." The important thing to recognize about this understandable phobia is that thorough preparation is the best antidote. The key to generating confidence is straight forward: prepare, prepare, prepare… and prepare some more. Adolescents can cultivate comfort with public speaking by asking at least one question in every class. Thousands of intrepid souls attend Toastmasters classes in America each year where they can hone their verbal skills in an environment geared toward helping them improve.

Outstanding orators challenge their listeners. During the dark days of the Civil War, President Lincoln would often seek to replenish his soul by listening to sermons by Dr. Finnes Gurley on Wednesday evenings at the New York Avenue Presbyterian Church. During the walk back to the White House one evening, an aide asked the President what he thought of the evening's message. Lincoln replied, "The content was excellent and delivered elegantly. It was clear that Dr. Gurley put a lot of effort into the sermon." The aide responded, "Then you thought it exceptional?" "No," said Lincoln. "It lacked the most important ingredient. He forgot to ask us to do something great."

There are many wonderful examples of leaders throughout history who have, however, inspired millions with their ability to verbally challenge and stir hearts and minds. President Lincoln was a master of this. He clearly articulated his vision for ending slavery while fighting to keep the nation united. Perhaps his most beloved speech, the Gettysburg Address, though a mere 266 words in length, is seared into the hearts of elementary school children, reminding us that clear, concise messages filled with meaningful content can resonate powerfully. Winston Churchill believed a speech should sound the way you talk, simple and conversational. He felt there was power in brevity. He would typically give a strong introduction, focus on one theme, provide vivid illustrations, and end emotionally. President John F. Kennedy's forceful eloquence galvanized an entire nation as he challenged citizens to "Ask not what your country can do for you, but ask what you can do for your country" and to commit the United States to be the "first nation to put a man on the moon and bring him back safely before the end of the decade." Martin Luther King, Jr. moved millions of Americans to care for one another through his charismatic calls for righteousness to reign. President Ronald Reagan will be remembered as one of our country's greatest leaders partly because of his authentic, winsome way of verbally communicating hope and pride in America.

3. **Written** - In today's fast paced world of technology we communicate more than ever through the written word. Emails, Twitter, Facebook, and texting are the overwhelming medium where thoughts are transmitted today. As convenient and expedient as these avenues are, they often also promote and forgive sloppy and inappropriately casual writing skills.

The ability to write well opens many avenues for a *Champion* to lead in an impactful way. The best way to learn to write is to write often. Schools, however, are giving short shrift to teaching writing skills because it is such a time-consuming endeavor to assess, correct, and provide constructive feedback on students' papers. Parents and teachers must focus less on these burdens and more on the benefits of maintaining high writing expectations to significantly help today's youth in evaluating writing. The good news is that written communication CAN be improved with repetition, evaluation, and feedback. While our goal should be to see this important skill get more attention in our classrooms, it is imperative to also practice and develop writing skills outside of, and in the years beyond, the classroom.

4. **Listening** - This is perhaps the least emphasized and developed of all communication skills and yet, perhaps the most important. Some have said that people listen at 25% of their total capacity. Imagine the valuable information we miss in our lifetimes, and all that could have been stored in our long term memory with a little more concentration.

To be a good listener takes work. Active listening is not easy or natural. Successful leaders carefully balance their natural propensity to be heard with their lesser desire to listen to others. People know if others are genuinely listening. The subtle message conveyed by bad listeners is "I don't have time for you" or "Whatever you are talking about is not important to me." Either message demonstrates a lack of respect and care for others. Authentic leaders blend humility with empathy, having a deep respect for the feelings and words of others.

Kent learned a valuable lesson about listening while dating his wife, Cindy. He noticed Cindy was an excellent listener with everyone she interacted with. She would actually remember what others said from previous conversations, while Kent self-deprecatingly noted he struggled to remember even the gist of what was shared. He was so impressed with her listening skills and appalled at his own that he purchased a book titled: *The Lost Art of Listening* by Michael Nichols. For him, the most poignant insight that Nichols offered was "if you are a good listener, you care more about the other person than you do yourself at the time you are interacting." That was Cindy. She cared more about Kent and others than she did herself when they were interacting. That is a rare pearl in a sea of societal self-absorption: *caring more about the other person than yourself,* which is exactly what lies in the hearts of the most respected and admired leaders!

The deliberate development and enhancement of communication skills has a potentially powerful rippling effect. The greatest communicators are messengers of hope, truth, and mercy. The absence of any one of those three virtues in any individual or relationship has anywhere from dysfunctional to dire consequences. *Champions for Life* have the communication skills to share truth, cultivate mercy, and inspire hope to help change the world through transforming lives!

# "Champions can Communicate"
### *Championship Points*

1. Good communication opens up doors in life.

2. Do not allow technology to diminish fundamental communication skills.

3. Listen with your eyes and ears.

4. To be a good listener requires sustained focus.

5. Avoid degrading language.

6. Speak greatness into the lives of others.

7. Never underestimate the power of nonverbal communication skills.

8. You never get a second chance to make a good first impression.

9. Make sure your actions and words are congruent.

# Chapter 10
## "Champions Foster a Culture of Unity"

*"Alone we can do so little; together we can do so much."*
(Helen Keller)

On a cold November night after an especially difficult season-ending loss to an archrival, a coach had an unusual dream. In it, he was transported to a building divided into two large rooms. Above the door leading into the first room was a sign that simply read, "Hell." As he approached the door it swung open slowly for him. Before he set foot inside he was struck by the sweet aroma coming from the room. Once inside, though, what he witnessed was tragic. Sitting around a large circular table were men and women reduced to virtual skeletons by starvation. It was worse than pictures he had seen of Nazi death camps. Their rags were tattered and food-stained, and their despair and desperation were overwhelming. In the middle of the table was some kind of delicious smelling stew so he couldn't understand why they were starving. As he looked closer he saw why. The only way they could reach the stew was with a six-foot long spoon. Each time they reached into the pot and filled up the spoon the process of trying to feed themselves ended in futility because their arms obviously weren't long enough to bring the food to their mouths. Every time they tried to eat, the stew would end up spilling on the floor or on their clothes. No person ever looked at their neighbor and no one even noticed he had entered the room because each was so consumed with trying to feed himself. None saw the sign painted on one of the walls that read ominously: "The Disease of Me has led to the Starvation of Us. Hell is the place where E.G.O. reigns supreme." He walked out badly shaken by what he had seen.

The coach then walked over to the door marked "Heaven." As the door opened for him, he could smell the same heavenly aroma that permeated Hell. He was surprised to find again a large circular table with the stew placed in the middle. Sitting around the table from the four corners of the earth were the healthiest, happiest collection of folks he had ever seen, laughing and enjoying each other's company. Those seated closest to him beckoned for the coach to join them at the table. He was shocked, however, to see that all of them also had six-foot long spoons to ladle out the heavenly smelling soup. But each time a person dipped their spoon in, instead of senselessly trying to bring it to their own mouths, they would offer it up to someone next to them. There was also a sign painted in this room and it read, "Heaven is a Place <u>W</u>ithout <u>E</u>qual." He also saw that the "W" and "E" were underscored. It struck him how one place was dominated and made joyful by "WE," while the other was brought to ruin by the disease of "ME." The coach asked a fellow if he knew what E.G.O. stood for? "Oh that," his new friend shared sadly, "stands for 'Edging God Out.'"

Unselfishness creates a powerful unity because it is rooted in caring, love, and mercy. As David writes in Psalm 133:1, "How good and pleasant it is when God's people live together in unity." When people unite in a common cause through helping others, their unity multiplies their strength. Legendary auto manufacturer Henry Ford believed that: "Coming together is a beginning. Keeping together is progress. Working together is success." Colonel Hal Moore, the combat leader so vividly portrayed by Mel Gibson in the movie, *We Were Soldiers*, created an acronym for the men trained under his command. W.E., he told them, stood for *Without Equal.* Their relentless training, their commitment to their cause, and most importantly their devotion to one another, he told them, would make them a fighting force literally without equal. Under conditions of extreme adversity in Vietnam facing an almost overwhelming enemy force, Colonel Moore's regiment truly fought with an uncommonly unselfish devotion that saved them from annihilation. In their training, Colonel Moore's troops came to understand the veracity of NBA coaching legend Pat Riley's insight, "The Disease of Me leads to the Defeat of Us." Or as Benjamin Franklin commented, "We must, indeed, all hang together or, most assuredly, we shall all hang separately." In the Lancer football program, Jim even made an acronym out of M.E., having it represent *Miss Everything,* as in we miss out on everything important in life when our primary focus is serving ourselves. Pastor Andy Stanley once humorously commented, "Whoever devotes themselves to themselves will have nothing but themselves to show for themselves." If you ever want to see a group literally consign itself to deflating underachievement where only insidious blame and excuse making flourish, examine a team or organization that has no unity.

Unselfishness, combined with a willingness to forgive, lies at the heart of unity. In modern times, nowhere was this demonstrated better on a large scale than Nelson Mandela's ascension to the presidency of South Africa after being unjustly imprisoned by a racist regime for 27 years. The natural impulse for retribution was set aside in favor of healing a nation on the verge of civil war. Nelson Mandela's understanding of the importance of unity was underscored in his autobiography, *Long Walk to Freedom*, where he admiringly shared an anecdote about an African leader who, "achieved the goal of all great leaders, he kept his people united." One of the critical lessons of Mandela's remarkable national achievement is that, ultimately, unity's strengths cannot be enjoyed unless mercy and forgiveness are present.

Forgiveness is the key to moving forward. Without it we remain mired in the past, weighed down by bitterness, resentment, and the memory of failures which often metastasize into debilitating regret. All of these detriments to success can be overcome by forgiveness. Forgiveness is the willingness to release resentment. Without the ability to forgive, a leader is trapped much like monkeys were by clever villagers in the following story. Along the west coast of India was a small village known for its prolific number and variety of monkeys. To supplement their subsistence farming, the locals would capture monkeys and sell them to zoo representatives. Over time, the young people in the community migrated to larger cities in search of better paying jobs. As the village's population aged, capturing the monkeys grew more difficult. Unable to afford expensive traps, the villagers devised a clever way to capture the primates. They tied a jar to a tree and put a cookie in the bottom of the jar. The jar's opening was barely big enough for the monkey's fist to push through. However, once the cookie was grabbed, the expanded monkey's fist was too big to extract, leaving it trapped. The only way to be free was to let go of the cookie. Forgiveness allowed President Mandela to help his people let go of the *cookie* trapping them, namely, the bitterness, anger, fear, and thirst for revenge that threatened to tear his nation apart. Applying that spiritually, we instinctively understand the truth behind the saying "he who cannot forgive others destroys the bridge over which he must pass." The Master Teacher Jesus put it this way, "If you don't forgive others, how do you expect your Heavenly Father to forgive you?"

Forgiveness is a powerful unifier in life. In January of 2011, Concordia University lost one of its female basketball players in a tragic car accident. The other three passengers who survived the accident were thankful their lives were spared but naturally grieved deeply for the young girl who lost her life. None of the survivors was more shattered than the young man driving the car. At the packed memorial service only days after the tragedy, many observed a remarkably rare act of human forgiveness. In the front row of the chapel sat the mother of the deceased young lady with her arm around the driver, comforting him throughout the service. That kind of forgiveness which is so unnatural and uncommon was witnessed because of the power of the one who unites all of humanity – Jesus Christ.

Hall of Fame Green Bay Packer Coach Vince Lombardi embraced the value of unity as he posited: "Build for your team a feeling of oneness, of dependence on one another and of strength to be derived by unity." Any principle or cause, such as unity, which raises the performance level of a team or organization, is considered to be a Force Multiplier. For example, take two basketball teams. We'll call them "Team A" and "Team B." Assigning ability values to the players and coaches for the two teams, we have the following:

|  | TEAM A | TEAM B |
| --- | --- | --- |
| POINT GUARD | 8 | 6 |
| SHOOTING GUARD | 7 | 7 |
| SMALL FORWARD | 9 | 6 |
| POWER FORWARD | 8 | 6 |
| CENTER | 9 | 7 |
| SIXTH MAN | 7 | 5 |
| COACHES | 7 | 8 |

If you add up the talents of each team's players and coaches, Team A scores higher with their composite total of 55, whereas Team B tallies 45. There is a substantial talent gap between the two. Given the difference between the two, Team B does not look to have a realistic chance to defeat Team A. However, the outcome will often depend on the Force Multipliers. If Team B has multipliers such as: motivation, unselfishness, work ethic, and unity – they have a higher probability for success. In this scenario, let's assume that Team A's Force Multiplier is a "7," while Team B's is substantially higher at a "9." Multiplying 55 times 7 yields 385, the real competitive value of Team A. Take the sum of the lesser talented Team B (45), but multiply it with a 9 because of its superior unity and you have a competitive value of 405. This is why some teams like the Duke University Blue Devils in basketball are so consistently competitive at an elite level year-in, year-out. Their talent may fluctuate somewhat from season to season, but their Force Multiplier is virtually always maximized at a 9 or 10. This perpetually gives them, or any organization that is highly unified, a competitive advantage regardless of opponents' talents or marketplace challenges.

Unselfishness does not mean we ignore our own self-interest. Rather it becomes the ultimate fulfillment of helping ourselves. We teach our athletes a simple formula: Greatness equals service. As Martin Luther King, Jr. noted, "anyone can be great because everyone can serve." Or as Jesus said: "Whoever wants to become great among you must be your servant" (Matthew 20:26). The paradox is true: "You cannot hold a torch to light another's path without brightening your own." This unselfishness, this deep-rooted desire and commitment to care for and forgive others, is foundational to the greatest competitive advantage any organization can possess, unity!

# "Champions Foster a Culture of Unity"
*Championship Points*

1. Unity is a Force Multiplier.

2. Unity is a primary goal of every great leader.

3. Highly unified organizations are without equal.

4. Unity is all about "us" rather than "me."

5. We miss out on the joy in life when we focus primarily on ourselves.

6. Lasting unity reflects unselfish love and eagerness to forgive others.

7. There is honor in putting others first.

8. Unification strengthens, division weakens.

# Chapter 11
## "Champions Strive to Rise Above Doom"

*"It takes 20 years to build a reputation and five minutes to **ruin** it. If you think about that, you'll do things differently."*
(Warren Buffett)

The pervading sentiment in society today is that success is measured by what you *have* in life. Success is often defined in quantitative terms such as owning a big home, driving a fast sports car, marrying the homecoming queen, inscribing impressive titles on business cards, coaching teams through undefeated seasons, or managing large stock portfolios. While there is nothing inherently wrong with money and fame, pursuing material things of this world might become addictive endeavors causing a loss of balance, perspective, and healthy priorities in life, ultimately leading to potential *doom*. Doom can strike like a sledgehammer, hard and without mercy. Doom, or unhappy ruin, is usually volitional with tragic consequences. Sadly, many admired icons have climbed hard to reach the rarified air of success only to experience severe embarrassment and hardships because of self-inflicted catastrophes that shattered their lives.

As we strive to become *Champions for Life* we must recognize the sobering reality that each of us is only one poor decision away from disaster. We all are similar to those who have experienced doom in their lives, in the sense we share an internal propensity for evil. Genesis 3:17 describes how we live in a flawed world with a systemic condition called sinful human nature. God said to Adam: "Because you listened to your wife and ate fruit from the tree about which I commanded you, 'you must not eat of it,' cursed is the ground because of you." The ground on which we live, the world in which we operate, is cursed because of our inherent sinfulness. In God's original design we were created to live in a world with no pain, disease, or failure. However, the world as we know it today continues to be flawed and in bondage due to man's sin and separation from God, dating all the way back to the Garden of Eden. However, the Good News is that God did not say "cursed are you Adam," but quite the contrary as we read in John 3:16, "For God so loved the world that He gave His one and only son, that whoever believes in Him shall not perish but have eternal life." The Gospel that Christians cling to provides hope in overcoming even the final despair of death. However, because the whole world is a prisoner to sin we must remain steadfastly vigilant to rise above potential doom.

There are many predictable temptations leading to doom. President Harry Truman once bluntly cautioned there are three things that ruin a man: "Power, money, and women [lust]." The Bible concurs with Truman's assessment, vividly describing the lives of numerous God-fearing leaders destroyed by foolish decisions. The lives of King Saul and King David for example, are tragic case studies of legendary leaders who began their careers as humble, noble servants unencumbered by obsession with their own personal agendas or resumes – but then DOOM!

Saul was the first appointed King over the people of Israel. He was impressive, blessed with good looks, image, mystique and style. His modesty garnered him widespread admiration and loyalty. Samuel, the prophet, boldly sang Saul's praises to all the people: "Do you see the man the Lord has chosen? There is no one like him among all the people. Then the people shouted, 'Long live the King!'" (1 Samuel 10:24). The public opinion polls of Saul skyrocketed even further after he won his first battle over the Ammonites. The pinnacle was reached!

Unfortunately, however, it didn't take long for Saul's life to unravel as the tempting allure of greed and insidious arrogance replaced the humility which had been the cornerstone of his character and appeal. The downward spiral of Saul's life accelerated with his insanely tormented jealousy of the military exploits of a rising warrior in the ranks by the name of David. The wise humility of Saul, which had placed him on such an honorable pedestal early in his leadership, turned into fearful paranoia and hatred, repulsing loyal followers and his loving family. After several failed attempts to kill David, Saul reached the valley of despair and committed suicide. What should have been the glory years of Saul's reign became dark and tragic.

The life of David, the shepherd boy warrior who slew Goliath, who initially became a revered king just like Saul, is again a study of how quickly the tide can turn in any life. The future king rose meteorically with unblemished promise in the minds of all Israel after courageously defeating the giant Philistine. The hero of his day, David received unparalleled praise and adulation. David was a champion warrior and leader until – DOOM! The prophet Samuel describes David's demise in 2 Samuel 11:2–3: "One evening David got up from his bed and walked around on the roof of the palace. From the roof he saw a woman bathing. The woman was very beautiful, **and** David sent someone to find out about her." This was just an ordinary night. David did not plan on courting disaster when he retired from a long day of hard work. Something stirred David from his slumber, perhaps tumbling in thought of tomorrow's duties or something as ordinary as answering nature's call, when he saw a beautiful woman next door bathing. If he would have just returned to bed to sleep, but the Bible records that dooming word **"and."** Samuel tells us that David saw a beautiful woman **and** made a decision to pursue his lust. **And** his life was never the same. He had set in motion a chain of events leading to his own inevitable destruction. David's desire for another man's wife cascaded unabated down on the king who was once honored for "having a heart after God." Fast forward to the present, and it is sad to report that unhealthy sexual proclivities are at an all-time high. Christian author and speaker James Dobson reports that "25% of the daily internet searches (68 million hits) access pornographic sites." Lust has historically been and continues to be a social cancer which inexorably corrodes the lives of leaders in families, business, sports, politics, and churches today.

Arrogance, greed, jealousy, and lust have wreaked havoc upon many successful people since Saul and David. The classic comedy duo Martin and Lewis broke up their act because of this "green-eyed monster" called jealousy. Kobe Bryant and Shaquille O'Neal predictably could have won a few more NBA championships with the Lakers had they been able to replace their envy with more humility. The "steroid era" of baseball could have been prevented if gifted athletes like Barry Bonds and Roger Clemens would have replaced their unbridled thirst for acclaim and achievement with a sense of thankfulness for the impressive talents they were both blessed with and forged through hard work.

There is one more human vice we dare not overlook as a factor which can flood our lives with misfortune. That is the sin of "anger." Many decisions have been blurred, games lost, relationships strained, and even lives lost because of succumbing to the temptation of permitting *controllable* emotions to escalate into fits of rage. There are sad stories that substantiate the truth that "Anger is only one letter short of Danger." We first spot the devastating effects of anger in Genesis 4:8: "Now Cain said to his brother Abel, 'Let's go out to the field.' While they were in the field, Cain attacked his brother Abel and killed him." Cain forfeited a peaceful relationship with his creator by allowing his insecurities to morph into such a violent state of mind that he actually murdered his brother. How could something this heinous happen? Paul reveals the answer in Ephesians 4:26: "In your anger do not sin. Do not let the sun go down while you are still angry, and do not give the devil a foothold." Anger in and of itself is not a sin. In fact, Jesus showed through driving the money changers out of the temple that anger may be justified. It is appropriate for us to become angry when observing injustice in the world. It is not sinful when our anger is directed at sin. However, Paul cautions when angry – "do not sin... do not give the devil a foothold." The problem arises when our anger surges over healthy barricades, allowing the devil to establish a beachhead where he prompts us into regrettable behaviors ranging from swearing, to road rage, to, as with Cain, murder.

One of the Bible's most heralded leaders ultimately experienced calamity because of his inability to control his anger. Moses, the humble deliverer of the Israelites, had a history of allowing his anger to surface. We read in Exodus 2:11-14 the first record of Moses "losing it":

> One day, after Moses had grown up, he went out to where his own people were and watched them at their hard labor. He saw an Egyptian beating a Hebrew, one of his own people. Glancing this way and that and seeing no one, he killed the Egyptian and hid him in the sand. The next day he went out and saw two Hebrews fighting. He asked the one in the wrong, 'Why are you hitting our fellow Hebrew?' The man said, 'Who made you ruler and judge over us? Are you thinking of killing me as you killed the Egyptian?' Then Moses was afraid and

thought, 'What I did must have become known.' When Pharaoh heard of this, he tried to kill Moses, but Moses fled from Pharaoh and went to live in Midian…

Moses was not carrying out a decree from the Lord to kill the Egyptian. He lost his composure. Because of this sin, he was forced to live his life as a fugitive.

A second time Moses' blood pressure rose to a boil occurred just after receiving the Ten Commandments on two stone tablets engraved by God's own hand. We read in Exodus 32:15-20:

> Moses turned and went down the mountain with the two tablets of the Testimony in his hands. They were inscribed on both sides, front and back. The tablets were the work of God; the writing was the writing of God, engraved on the tablets… When Moses approached the camp and saw the calf and the dancing, **his anger burned** and he threw the tablets out of his hands, breaking them to pieces at the foot of the mountain. And he took the calf they had made and burned it in the fire; then he ground it to powder, scattered it on the water and made the Israelites drink it.

Moses understandably became enraged with the Israelites' abominable worshipping of a golden calf. He shattered God's sacred tablets and punished the Hebrews by forcing them to drink the water laden with the idol's powdered remains. While Moses' action may not have been a sin, God drew attention to the fact that Moses had to climb Mt. Sinai a second time to receive a replacement set of Commandments: "The Lord said to Moses, 'Chisel out two stone tablets like the first ones, and I will write on them the words that were on the first tablets, **which you broke'**" (Exodus 34:1). God did not chastise Moses for his actions, but drew attention to the fact that his tirade caused him to break the first tablets. (Kent can only imagine what God would have liked to have told him during his adolescence when he was buying a new tennis racquet to replace the mangled one in the trash can or when he threatened to throw his golf clubs to the bottom of Wilshire Lake!)

The final recorded display of anger from Moses was highly

significant, unfortunately producing lasting negative ramifications. Before describing this event it is important to remember that Moses was not a raging lunatic. In fact, Moses was so esteemed by God he met with Him at the burning bush to give Moses his "marching orders" for the greatest leadership assignment in history, freeing the Israelites from bondage in Egypt. In Numbers 12:3, we learn how God viewed Moses: "Moses was a very humble man, more humble than anyone else on the face of the earth." However, Moses was also human and could not completely rise above his propensity for unhealthy anger. That doomsday for Moses began with the usual litany of complaints from the thirsty Israelites. Moses beseeched the Lord for help and received the following command: **"Speak to that rock** before their eyes and it will pour out its water" (Numbers 20: 8-12). God's instructions were clear, but on this day, Moses' impatience with his fellow Israelites boiled over. Standing with his brother Aaron in front of the rock after gathering everyone, he lambasted them with these words: "'**Listen, you rebels**, must **WE** bring you water out of this rock?' Then Moses raised his arm and **struck the rock twice** with his staff. Water gushed out, and the community and their livestock drank." Moses had become indignant at the people's incessant complaining and because of his frustration erroneously took credit for causing the rock to gush water. Moses was a good man who had done so much to serve the Lord. It is understandable that Moses was infuriated with the lack of faith of the Israelites and their chronic tendency to complain. However, as is so often the case with anger, one poorly chosen phrase and one bad action precipitated doom. God had forgiven and overlooked Moses' previous bouts of anger, but this one would produce a dire consequence as recorded in Numbers 20:12: "The Lord said to Moses and Aaron, 'Because you did not trust in me enough to honor me as holy in the sight of the Israelites, you will not bring this community into the land I give them.'" Sadly, Moses would never enter the Promised Land he had been wandering towards for 40 years.

Because we are human, anger is difficult to avoid. The challenge is not to let the devil get a foothold and subsequently do or say things that hurt ourselves or anyone else. This is easy to pledge, but difficult to achieve. That is why we see the harmful effects of anger in the lives of so many respected leaders. For example, General

George Patton's incredible leadership record and reputation were forever tarnished after the following incident occurred on August 10, 1943:

> While visiting wounded soldiers in the army hospital Patton encountered a private without wounds. When asked by Patton why he was there, he replied, "I guess I just can't take it anymore, Sir. The shelling is too much for me." Patton went into a rage, swearing obscenities, hitting the man twice with his fists on the head, and waving his pistol at him, threatening to kill him.

The revered football coach of the Ohio State Buckeyes, Woody Hayes, who amassed an impressive 238-72-10 record winning four National Championships and 13 Big Ten titles ultimately forfeited his job because of his inability to control his anger. The public and Buckeye administration for years patiently overlooked Coach Hayes' temper. In 1971 he broke sideline markers in the final minute of a loss to Michigan on National TV, and in 1973 shoved a camera into the eye of a camera man before the Rose Bowl. In 1977, he punched an ABC cameraman during a loss to Michigan. Finally, Coach Hayes' anger sunk him when he lost his job after punching a Clemson football player in the 1978 Gator Bowl.

The history books, divorce courts, principals' offices, and police blotters record numerous turbulent episodes of self-inflicted doom imposed by the inability to control anger. It is difficult, but it is possible to manage this ubiquitous foe. God wishes for us to live our lives with peace and poise rather than with angry outbursts. James encourages us and puts this quest in perspective: "My dear brothers, take note of this: Everyone should be quick to listen, slow to speak and slow to become angry, for man's anger does not bring about the righteous life that God desires" (James 1:19-20).

As *Champions for Life* we strive to honor God by our daily decisions and service to others. We are all called to be ever vigilant to intentionally protect ourselves from temptations that can cause irreparable harm to our reputations, family, friends, and careers. However, as hard as we try, it is impossible to completely shield ourselves from the sin that desires to consume us and bring shame to our lives in a fallen world. The apostle Paul captures our ongoing struggle in Romans 7:18-19: "I know that nothing good lives in me, that is, in my sinful nature. For I have the desire to do what is good, but I cannot carry it out. For what I do is not the good I want to do; no, the evil I do not want to do - this I keep on doing." Paul was an expert on traps in life that nurture doom. The good news is that God, in his infinite wisdom and mercy, knew we could never fully avoid sinning so He sacrificed His Son Jesus Christ to save us from this devouring sin. We have assurance of the forgiveness of our sins and eternal life because of the suffering, death, and resurrection of Jesus.

Fortunately, there are examples of Bible heroes who did not fall off the moral precipice such as Joseph, Joshua, and Daniel, each of whom is worthy of study and emulation. Joseph refused to yield to the seductive wiles of Potiphar's wife, choosing instead to *flee* from a temptation which would have produced certain catastrophe and kept him from reaching his full potential as a leader. It is a simple concept, to "flee" when the allure of temptations is so intoxicating. If King David would have "fled" back to his own bed alone rather than calling for the beautiful Bathsheba, his life and leadership would have never been ripped apart by dishonorable behavior. Champions in athletics are often recognized for being "fleet of foot." *Champions for Life* are known for keeping their eyes riveted on Christ to maintain the conviction to rise above temptations and flee from the pitfalls of impending doom!

# Champions Strive to Rise above Doom
*Championship Points*

1. Doom is self-inflicted when values are abandoned or ignored.

2. Know that temptations are inevitable.

3. Adversity can occur even when doing everything right.

4. In the face of overwhelming temptation – flee!

5. Surround yourself with honorable people of sterling integrity.

6. Know that greed, lust, and anger act as quicksand for personal lives and professional careers.

7. When adversity strikes, remember that God is bigger than any event or circumstance.

8. Regardless of past mistakes, never forget that Jesus Christ is eager to forgive and forget!

# Chapter 12
Champions Influence Others

*"There is no power on earth that can neutralize the influence of a high, simple and useful life."*

(Booker T. Washington)

It was a beautiful spring day in 1974. Two runners were on base with two outs in the bottom of the 7th inning with the Denver Lutheran Lights trailing by one run. A simple base hit wins the ball game. It wasn't just any game, it was Mr. Kettner's chance at a career 100th victory. Kent had enjoyed playing for this legendary baseball coach during the final three years of his high school career and, like all the students, had enormous respect and honor for this beloved mentor. The pitcher wound up and threw his first pitch and Kent swung and missed. Mr. Kettner could be spotted in his familiar pose along the third base line uttering his familiar words of encouragement: "That's okay Slick, it just takes one – Hubba, Hubba!" The second pitch was met with another swing and a miss followed by: "This is the one Slick – Hubba, Hubba!" The typical 17-year-old adolescent longing for acceptance and acclaim, wanted to hit the ball not only to boost a fragile sense of self-confidence, but also to help win the milestone game for the favorite male in his life next to his dad. The third pitch seemed to cross the plate faster than the previous two and Kent struck out swinging. It was a long walk to the dugout and an even longer walk to the locker room for the "loser." Kent cannot recall one word uttered following the game, but vividly remembers sitting on a curb in the parking lot feeling like he had let many people down. Decades later, Kent can still vividly recall Mr. Kettner walking slowly to his car and driving out of the parking lot to go home and then, for some reason, making a U-turn and driving back to where Kent was sitting. Mr. Kettner got out of his car, leaving the engine running and walked up to Kent with his hand warmly extended saying: "Slick, tomorrow is another day, keep smiling Smiley." After those brief healing and caring words, Mr. Kettner got back in his car and drove home. On that spring day, a respected leader took time to convey to a young adolescent "loser" that he was "okay." Life has many seminal moments where people's destinies are forever changed, just like in this situation for Kent. When Kent was at his most vulnerable, a disappointed look or critical remark from his respected leader would have crushed a youngster already reeling from, in his mind, letting his beloved coach and teammates down. Instead, Mr. Kettner, a paragon of kindness and virtue, offered a hand of redemption, hope, and love to a boy who he knew desperately needed those things.

The shaping of character and the coming to clarity of life's purpose is achieved through the humble influence of parents, teachers, coaches, pastors, and neighbors. The great irony is that these leaders seldom realize the depth of the impact they are making. In retrospect for Kent, it was through the events of that crisp spring day and the traumatic strike out, that he began to clearly sense his calling in life was to be a teacher and coach after experiencing the powerfully positive influence of his humble hero. As a wise anonymous sage once posited, "Influence may be the highest of human skills."

Renowned author and speaker John Maxwell states unequivocally that *"Leadership is Influence."* It is easy to see that a person can have a positive or negative influence on the people they interact with daily. We encourage those who strive to be *Champions for Life* to dedicate themselves to making a positive difference in the lives of each person they encounter. This noble pursuit was on the tongue of Jesus Christ when He commanded the disciples to "Go ye therefore and teach all nations, baptizing them in the name of the Father, and of the Son, and of the Holy Spirit" (Matthew 28:19). This Great Commission to make disciples is the ultimate eternal influence a person can have helping others by the power of the Holy Spirit to embrace the saving grace offered through the atoning death and resurrection of Jesus.

There are many ways to have a positive influence on other people. Influence begins with deliberately pursuing excellence in all that we do in life. We live in a world today satisfied with mediocrity. You don't have to look hard to find leaders just going through the motions to produce *satisfied* customers rather than seizing the opportunity to create *Raving Fans*. Ken Blanchard, one of America's top business mentors asserts that raving fan excellence is obtainable in the workplace today with a little more effort on small details and applying the Golden Rule. CEOs at companies such as In-N-Out Burger, Chick-Fil-A, Ritz Carlton, Toyota, and Nordstrom know that hard work and attention to details lead to an excellent product and experience for customers that will perpetuate future success. Excellence within these raving fan organizations becomes almost palpable everywhere you turn.

There is an important correlation worth noting between a leader's pursuit of excellence and their credibility. As the *excellence* of an organization is heightened, the *credibility* of that organization is also increased in the eyes of the public. The record of UCLA basketball under the leadership of Coach Wooden was unlike any other in college history. Leadership and life principles espoused by Coach Wooden remain today highly prized in the eyes of millions in part because of the unprecedented aura of excellence associated with UCLA basketball from 1948 to 1975. The success enjoyed by the Bruins was one indicator of the high credibility of their leader. All who were ever fortunate enough to meet this legendary leader or hear him speak became enamored with the exemplary character which made him a personal paragon even beyond his record as a coach.

The overarching benefit of pursuing excellence and becoming a credible leader within your field, is that as *excellence* is realized and *credibility* is earned, then one's opportunity to have significant *influence* is expanded. The platform to speak from and make a difference in the lives of others is far greater for those known for excellence compared to those who wallow in mediocrity. There are going to be more requests to hear a coach who has a record of 30-2 as opposed to 2-30. Leaders from successful companies that make an excellent product or create an unforgettable experience for their customers are frequently asked to share ideas with others because of their perceived high level of credibility.

The relationship that exists between *Excellence - Credibility - Influence* is important for leaders to embrace. Resources of time, money, and energy must be expended in key areas to help foster excellence within an organization. Duke University is today one of the most selective universities in the world and recognized as one of the elite colleges in the country. After touring the beautiful campus in Durham, North Carolina it is evident why, with so many esteemed professors, it is an academic juggernaut. However, the area that receives the most notoriety in the eyes of millions across the country is the excellence acclaimed in basketball under the leadership of Mike Krzyzewski. The ability of this *credible* Duke University to *influence* lives today is at an all-time high largely because of Coach K's magnificent program.

Excellence, like beauty, is hard to define, but is easy to recognize. So it is with trying to quantify steps that make an organization excellent. There is no simple formula for excellence that can be easily replicated. If excellence was easy to achieve, everyone would have gold medals. The good news is that reaching a state of excellence is not rocket science either. The universal truth about excellence can be captured in the following truism: "The difference between ordinary and extraordinary is that little extra." The hard work necessary to provide that little extra is unfortunately a rare commodity in the world today. *Champions* recognize that to influence others in a positive manner they must embrace hard work and have a personal affinity for excellence. Eleanor Roosevelt drives this point home remarking, "You can never really live anyone else's life, not even your child's. The influence you exert is through your own life, and what you've become yourself."

As we examine leaders today we can identify those who are obviously effective and those who are not. In striving to be exemplary leaders, two simple reference points can measure the effectiveness of our quest to influence individual lives or organizations. First, great leaders show a high degree of *prudence* or good judgment in their decision making. When leaders do **foolish** things, they lose their reputation as prudent leaders able to consistently make good choices and decisions. Second, memorable leaders show a high commitment to *ethics* consisting of a good value system. When leaders make **unethical** choices, their reputation suffers potentially irreparable damage. Leaders must humbly realize that the public monitors their performance and behavior and continually evaluates their effectiveness based upon these two reference points.

Perfection is not required to be a *Champion*. However, accepting responsibility when mistakes are made is critical to maintaining one's honor, focus, and credibility. *Champions* may fall, but it is essential to not blame others or make excuses and instead to accept responsibility and move forward. Leaders who never admit to error lose credibility and demonstrate a lack of integrity.

The public can forgive a lack of prudence much more easily than when ethical errors are made. When leaders make dumb mistakes, the public can accept a lack of prudence particularly if an apology follows the error. For example, in June of 2010, major league umpire Jim Joyce called a runner "safe" at first base though televised replays showed that he had clearly blown the call and the runner was actually "out." This routine call was not just any call, it was potentially the 27th out for Armando Galarraga who had pitched a perfect game for the Detroit Tigers until the runner at first was erroneously called "safe." Joyce's poor decision denied Galarraga a rarified place in Major League history. Once Jim Joyce saw the replays, he was devastated by his lack of prudence at a crucial time and thoughtfully apologized to Galarraga following the game. The umpire had security protect his family for a few days after the game because he predicted that he would be excoriated by the media and potentially attacked by fans for his blunder. Joyce was pleasantly surprised to find the pundits had tempered their criticism once they had learned of his apology to Galarraga and could sense his genuine remorse.

When a leader demonstrates a lack of ethics or weak value system, the public is much more harsh and critical in response. Richard Nixon's and Bill Clinton's popularity as American Presidents never returned to the zeniths they once enjoyed after their dishonest and moral mistakes made while in office. Athletes who cheat to win notoriety or scandalously cheat on their spouses lose legions of fans, accolades, and respect. The betrayal of recognized virtues and standards undermines the potential benefit of being leaders – true champions – despite talents and notoriety. Ethical mistakes bring more severe and lasting damage to a leader's reputation. Doing "wrong things" as a leader shows grave character weakness and results in a substantial loss of credibility and trust.

The word credibility comes from the Latin word *credo* which means "I believe." A creed in the Christian Church is a statement of what the members believe to be true regarding God. A *credit* card company loans millions of people money to buy items because they *believe* people will pay them back for the money loaned to them. A *credible* leader is one whose followers believe in and trust. John Wooden was *believable* because his actions and his words were congruent and many more of his decisions were wise rather than foolish. There are far more leaders today who lack credibility because of errors of prudence and/or ethics or because their actions lack any consistent application of core beliefs and principles. *Champions for Life* understand the relationship between these two important reference points and the impact on their reputations as credible leaders.

People are an organization's only sustainable competitive advantage. Without excellent people it is an exercise in self-deception to claim to be good or claim to be making the enormously difficult transition of *Good to Great*, a transformative process so well dissected and analyzed in Jim Collins' book by the same title. Dan Cathy, the president of Chick-Fil-A restaurants, asserts that leaders of great organizations differentiate their organization from the competition. The sustained competitive advantage for Chick-Fil-A begins behind the counter where Cathy contends that the "leaders must first take care of their employees before the employees are going to go the extra mile with customers." This eagerness to go the "extra mile" with people is a subtle difference between mediocrity and excellence, and one that begins with the leader. There is no greater compliment or indictment of leadership than the quality of the people who comprise the organization and the care given to them.

For quality people to flourish within an organization requires the leader to operate from a "Servant Paradigm." In James' Hunter's book, *The Servant*, he shares there are only two bases for leadership. One is power, the ability to force or coerce someone to do their will because of the title they possess. Leaders from this mold build very hierarchical organizations heavily dependent on title and policy. Their demeanors can vary widely from brusque, domineering, and dictatorial to firm to pleasant. But regardless of personality or style, a centralized decision-making process and bureaucratized control is usually the norm. Power-based leaders struggle creating and promulgating vision, replace relationships with formal committees and policies, and unintentionally stifle the creative and productive juices of their best people. Sometimes they are micro-managers, but almost always feel compelled and responsible for making every key decision that will affect the organization. Lack of self-confidence is often at the root of why leaders are reluctant to empower others and instead stifle others within an organization. Over time, the net result of the undiluted and consistent exercise of power is a decline in morale and subsequent decline in productivity. There is little recognition by power leaders of their responsibility to develop their followers because their focus is constantly on directing them. Power-based leaders lack the self-awareness to realize they are inadvertently closing out the very talents that could make both the organization and them shine.

The antithesis of the power-based model is one centered on the development and utilization of authority. Hunter defines authority as the ability to get someone to do your will because they choose to in response to your clear desire to consistently help, develop, serve, and honor them. The leader who has authority need not lord it over anyone; they have built a large bank account of trust and respect with those they lead through subordinating themselves to serving an exhilarating vision and the principle values that all have embraced. People need to be inspired to pursue a vision that will make their spirits soar while girding them from caving in to daunting challenges or obstacles. They need to know and believe they are improving and growing. People excel in a climate that embraces the individual and their personal involvement in continuous improvement. When leaders empower individual workers to actively become involved in making decisions, they gain freedom and personal ownership to help the organization excel. Creating a climate of "Kaizen" and resourcing an individual's opportunity for growth produces an energized environment. Empowering individuals to make decisions in essence makes them vital stewards for the organization and gives them a stake in the organization they are proud to embrace and reluctant to abandon.

Authority-based leaders allow their prioritized core values to guide the organization while their people experience an exciting freedom to produce within those boundaries. These types of leaders view themselves as stewards rather than owners or directors. They understand that the people who work with them are essentially on "loan" to the organization rather than indentured servants. They are to be nurtured and sharpened, treasured for their gifts and held accountable for fully utilizing them. Ultimately, authority is acquired through serving and sacrificing for those we lead. It is strengthened when followers see the leader's subordination to honorable values and a worthy purpose. It is cemented when organizational members realize that their leaders have their best interests at heart.

On April 18, 1920, Paul Leonard Briggs was born in Providence, Rhode Island. His mother was a French nurse and his father a Harvard educated engineer. As a young boy, Paul became fascinated with the game of football. His family's apartment overlooked the Brown University practice field, and young Paul would spend hours watching the Bears practice. One afternoon when he was 10 years old, his mother observed: "Paul, you are really fascinated by this game of football, aren't you?" He responded, "Mom, you see those 22 fellas out there. I'm going to be one of them someday. And you see the man in the suit, that's Coach Tuss McLauhery, and one day I'm going to be a coach just like him!"

From the time he was 10 years old, Paul Briggs had a clarity about his purpose in life. Later he would say he had four goals and allegiances that governed his existence; Devotion to Country, Love of Family, Commitment to Football, and Acceptance of his Lord. He wasted no time or energy on anything that did not fall within those four parameters. He was married to his beloved wife, Sally, for 63 years until her death in 2010. He enlisted in the Navy during World War II, rising to the rank of Commander winning the Bronze Star, Purple Heart, and many more medals while fighting in fierce battles throughout the Pacific. After the war he continued to serve in the Naval Reserves for 37 years. He became an All-American offensive and defensive tackle at the University of Colorado before playing for the Detroit Lions in the NFL. After his professional career ended, he coached high school and college football for 57 years. He was the National Coach of the Year in 1971, spoke on the lecture circuit with Bear Bryant and Adolf Rupp, and led Bakersfield High School into becoming the all-time winningest program in the history of California football.

Coach Briggs was larger than life, and his influence has already spanned generations. Over 3,000 young men played under him, and all were deeply impacted. Of a handful of the greatest coaches of all eras, it can be rightly stated that their teams won so frequently not so much because of what they did but rather because of the values engraved in the hearts of their coaches. As a motivational figure and speaker, he was unparalleled. Clarity, courage, commitment, honor, loyalty, passion, service, truth, and toughness were the seeds he planted and the values he emblazoned on the 3,000 young men that his Lord placed in his path. Coach Briggs was one of the "Greatest Generation's" warriors who joined thousands of other brave soldiers to help save the world from barbarous tyranny. On February 14, 2011, Coach Briggs was reunited with his Lord and beloved wife Sally. But before he entered his Heavenly home he spent 57 seasons altering destinies. From his bravery at Iwo Jima to his coaching inspiration at Bakersfield High School, his influence will echo heroically throughout eternity because he was the consummate *Champion for Life*!

Nearly 2500 years ago, the great Athenian statesman Pericles shared this with grieving family members honoring war dead: "What you leave behind is not what is engraved in stone monuments, but what is woven into the lives of others." Leaders like Coach Kettner and Coach Briggs were *champions* of the highest character who influenced countless lives and left legacies that will continue for generations. Dedicated individuals who follow timeless leadership principles with a clear vision and commitment of weaving positive values into their own hearts and the hearts of others will undoubtedly become and create *Champions for Life*.

# "Champions Influence Others"
### *Championship Points*

1. Champions always look to make a positive impact in the lives of others.

2. We influence through the pursuit and acquisition of excellence.

3. Mediocrity is lamentable and forgettable while excellence is laudable and memorable.

4. Reputations shrink with foolish choices and are sunk with unethical behavior.

5. Credibility is a cornerstone of trustworthy leadership.

6. Develop authority with others by serving them.

7. Avoid lording the power of your position over others.

8. *Champions for Life* leave an indelible mark on others; their selfless legacy reverberates throughout the ages.

# Notes

## Preface

p. ix     Orange Lutheran Lancers vs. Mater Dei Monarchs football game on September 7, 2003. Orange Lutheran won 35-14.

p. xi     Hebrews 12:1 (The Holy Bible, New International Version. 1984. International Bible Society)

p. xi     John 14:6 (The Holy Bible, New International Version. 1984. International Bible Society)

p. xi     John 8:12 (The Holy Bible, New International Version. 1984. International Bible Society)

## Introduction

p. xiii     Integrity comes from the Latin derivation "integritas." (Merriam Webster Dictionary)

p. xiv     *Machte Virtute* by Coach Jim Tressel – Former Ohio State football coach's team room as observed by Jim Kunau during visit with coach.

p. xiv     "There is nothing noble in being superior…" (https://www.brainyquote.come)

p. xv     Coach Wooden – "Peace of mind which is the direct result…" (*A Game Plan for Life* by Don Yaeger, 2009, New York: Bloomsbury. P. 23).

p. xv     Coach Bob Ladoceur - "Kids will fight for you if you stand for more…" (*When the Game Stands Tall* by Neil Hayes. 2003. North Atlantic: Berkely, CA, P. 11)

p. xv     Coach Joe Ehrmann - *Season of Life* (Marx, J. 2003. New York: Simon & Schuster).

## Chapter #1: Face God First

p.1     Never be afraid to trust an unknown future to a known God." Corrie Ten Boom – (https://www.brainyquote.com)

p. 2     The Bombardier Beetle (insects.about.com)

p. 2    Genesis 1:1 (The Holy Bible, New International Version. 1984. International Bible Society)

p. 3    Story of Louis Zamperini: (*Unbroken* by Laura Hillenbrand (2010). New York: Random House)

p. 4    John 8:32 (The Holy Bible, New International Version. 1984. International Bible Society)

p. 4    Exodus 3:1-4 (The Holy Bible, New International Version. 1984. International Bible Society

p. 5    "Mother Teresa reported that she still began each day …. (http://www.shalem.org/index.php/resources/publications/articles -written-by-shalem-staff/contemplative-possibilities-in-worship- by-tilden-edwards).

p. 5    Mother Teresa – "a little pencil in the hand…" (*Mother Teresa* by Kathryn Spink. 1997.   San Francisco: Harper Collins.)

p. 6    Canadian Coast Guard and American Sea Captain is a fictitious story told on numerous internet sites.

p. 6    C.S. Lewis (*A Grief Observed* by C.S. Lewis. 1967. New York: Harper Collins).

p. 7    Footprint poem by Mary Stevenson: "One night I dreamed I was walking along the beach with the Lord…" (http://www.footprints-inthe-sand.com/)

p. 8    I Kings 3:5-9 (The Holy Bible, New International Version. 1984. International Bible Society)

p. 8    Joseph Scriven in 1855… *What a Friend We Have in Jesus.* (http://www.raymondscountydownwebsite.com/html/joseph_scri ven.ht)

p. 9    Hebrews 11:1 (The Holy Bible, New International Version. 1984. International Bible Society)

p. 10   II Chronicles 16:9 (The Holy Bible, New International Version. 1984. International Bible Society)

p. 10   "…St. Augustine reminds us, is to one day see what we believe." (http://www.positive-thinking-principles.com/quotes-about faith.html)

p. 11   Matthew 6:33 (The Holy Bible, New International Version. 1984. International Bible Society)

**Chapter 2: Champions Have Strong Character**

p. 12 - "Waste no more time arguing what a good man should be, be one." (Marcus Aurelius) - https://dailystoic.com

p. 12    Story of Warren Buffet – (*Faith in the Game* by Tom Osborne. 1999. Broadway Books: New York, NY. p. 2)

p. 12    Greek philosopher Heraclitus asserts: "A person's character …" (http://www.ashbrook.org/publicat/oped/moore/04/character.html

p. 13    George Washington: "In all my endeavors I have sought…" (*The Founding Fathers on Leadership* by Donald Phillips. 1997. Warner Books: New York, NY. P. 49)

p. 13    Teddy Roosevelt: "To educate a man in mind, but not in…." (http://thinkexist.com/quotation/to_educate_a_man_in_mind_and _not_in_morals_is_to/346791.html)

p. 13    Helen Keller: "Character cannot be developed in ease and quiet…" (http://www.rsds.org/1/publications/review_archive/lessons_learn ed.htm).

p. 15    Tom Osborne: "Dallas Cowboy's Coach Tom Landry often said he…" (https://leoadambiga.com/2016/10/27living-legend-tom-osborne-still winning-game-of-life-at-79/amp/

p. 15    General MacArthur: "Too late." (*No Substitute for Victory, Lessons in Strategy and Leadership from General Douglas MacArthur* by Theodore and Donna Kinne. 2005. Prentice Hall: New Jersey. P. 6)

p. 16    Ben Franklin: "I never knew a man …" (http://www.eastwallingfordbaptist.com/INSPIRATIONAL%20 QUOTES.htm).

p. 16    The word "Character" comes from the Greek meaning – "to engrave." (http://www.thefreedictionary.com/character)

p. 16    Dr. Martin Luther King: "You may be 38 years old …." (Excerpt from Dr. Marin Luther King's sermon at Ebeneezer Baptist Church in 1967, Atlanta, GA)

p. 17    1 Corinthians 15:33 (The Holy Bible, New International Version. 1984. International Bible Society)

p. 17    The story of Edwin and John Wilkes Booth was compiled after reading numerous documents about the lives of these two men.

p. 18    Tony Dungy (*Uncommon: Finding Your Path to Significance* by Tony Dungy. 2009. Tyndale House Publishers: Carol Stream, IL.

P. 4)


p. 19     Professor Cornelius Platinga describes scriptural wisdom as the knowledge of God's creation…
(http://dailychristianquote.com/dcqplantinga.html)

p. 19     Integrity – integritas – "whole, entire, complete."
(http://www.thefreedictionary.com/integrity)

p. 20     David Gergen: "Character without capacity usually means weakness…"
(http://www.itoa.org/leadership_paper/leadershippart_II.pdf).

p. 20     Rudy Giuliani: "You've got to build yourself up for the terrible things that are going to happen…."
(http://articles.ocregister.com/2010-02
17/cities/24650490_1_motivational-speaker-rudolph-giuliani-
seminar).

p. 21     Pat Williams: "you must prepare yourself ahead of time…."
(*Coaching Your Kids to be Leaders* by Pat Williams. 2005. New York: Time Warner Book Group. P. 156).

p. 21     Billy Graham: "… the only thing that happens when your wrestle with a pig…."(paraphrased from ---
http://www.ccel.us/billy.ch26.html)

p. 21     Philippians 4:8 (The Holy Bible, New International Version. 1984. International Bible Society)

p. 21     "In ancient Babylon, one day the king summoned all his wisest counselors…."
(http://www.crossroads-crc.org/newsfile14424_2.pdf).

p. 22     Chuck Colson: (*How Now Shall We Live* by Chuck Colson. 1999. Illinois: Tyndale House Publisher).

p. 23     Boris Pasternak: "We have to understand our attitude toward existence…"
(http://ministryvalues.com/index.php?option=com_content&task
=view&id=1016&Itemid=34).

p. 23 Andy Stanley: "Character as the will to do what is right, as defined by God…."
(http://www.sermoncentral.com/sermons/uncompromised-
character-tim-smithsermon-on-jesus-christ-129617.asp)

p. 23     Theodore Roosevelt: "Character in the long run, is the decisive factor in the life of an individual…."
(http://www.amnh.org/common/faq/quotes.html)

**Chapter 3: Champions Exhibit Humility**

p. 26    "The best leaders are usually humble leaders..." John Wooden (https://www.brainyquotecom)

p. 26    Matthew 11:28-29 (The Holy Bible, New International Version. 1984. International Bible Society)

p. 26    Story of Naaman – 2 Kings 5 (The Holy Bible, New International Version.1984. International Bible Society)

p. 27    Proverbs 27:2 (The Holy Bible, New International Version. 1984. International Bible Society)

p. 27    *The Indispensible Man* poem written by Saxon White Kessinger in 1959 can be found at: (http://www.appleseeds.org/indispen-man_saxon.htm).

p. 28    Lou Holtz – "the biggest room in the world…." mobile.twitter.com

p. 28    Information about Kansas State University Football and Coach Bill Snyder summarized from the following: (*Bill Snyder; They Said it Couldn't be Done.* 2006. Illinois: KCI Sports).

p. 29    *The Purpose Driven Life* by Rick Warren. 2002. Michigan: Zondervan.

p. 30    The story of the Roman Centurion and Jesus summarized from Matthew 8:5-13. (The Holy Bible, New International Version. 1984. International Bible Society)

p. 30    St. Augustine: "Faith is to believe what you do not see…" mobile.brainyquote.com

p. 31    John Wooden: "…greatest joy definitely comes from doing …." https//www.brainyquote.com

p. 31    Harry Truman: "It is amazing what you can accomplish when…" (*The Power of Nice* by Linda K. Thaler & Robin Koval. 2006. Double Day).

p. 31    Story of Sara Tucholsky summarized from newspaper accounts and video clips.

p. 32    George Washington: "I beg they will accept my cordial thanks…" (http://www.loc.gov/teachers/classroommaterials/presentationsan dactivities/presentations/timeline/amrev/contarmy/accepts.html). - https://www.thewoodedeffect.com

p. 36    "A vision is not just a picture of what could be ..." Rosabeth Moss Kanter (https://www.brainyquote.com)

p. 36    Viktor Frankl, *Man's Search For Meaning*. 1984. Simon & Schuster: New York

p. 37    Author Pat Williams: "Vision is the ability to make the future happen…"

p. 36    Proverbs 29:18 "Without Vision the People Perish." King James Version

p. 37    Shakespeare's Hamlet: "This above all: to thine own self be true…" (https://www.nosweatshakespeare.com)

p. 37    Coach Wooden: "Throughout my career I did not allow others to make me adopt…"
(*Wooden on Leadership* by John Wooden & Steve Jamison. 2005.
New York: McGraw –Hill. P. 57)

p. 38    Luke 16:13 (The Holy Bible, New International Version. 1984. International Bible Society)

p. 38    "President Reagan's greatness derives in large part…" (*Ronald Reagan* by Dinesh D'zousa. 1997. Touchstone: New York.)

p. 38    Coach Gary Barnett: "We're going to take the Purple to Pasadena."
(*High Hopes* by Gary Barnett. 1996. New York: Warner Books. P. 18).

p. 38    Coach Mike Krzyzewski: "… set of core inflexible principles: communication, trust…."
(*Leading With the Heart* by Mike Krzyzewski. 2000. New York: Business Plus).

p. 38    Lunch meeting with Coach John Wooden took place on October 12, 2006 just three days before his 96th birthday. Interesting to note that on his birthday on October 14th, a Post Office in Reseda, California was named in his honor.

p. 39    Coach Wooden sagely explains: "When leaders instill the belief…." (*Wooden on Leadership* by John Wooden and Steve Jamison. 2005. McGraw-Hill: New York. P. 179

p. 39    Chinese proverb: "If your vision is for a year, plant wheat…."
(http://www.purposequest.com/assets/pdfs/misc/creativity/succes Quotes.pdf).

p. 39   According to John Maxwell, Sociologists believe that the most introverted people will influence 10,000 others in an average lifetime.
(http://www.leadershipmoment.org/site/c.egLNI0OCKrF/b.4101 065/k.871F/Leadership_FAQs.htm).

p. 40   Blue Ocean Strategy vs. Red Ocean
(Harvard Business Review. W. Chan Kim & Renee A. Mauborgne.
12 pages. Publication date: Oct 01, 2004. Prod. #: R0410D-PDF-ENG).

p. 41   George Barna defines leadership as "motivating, mobilizing, resourcing, and directing people…." (*A Fish Out of Water* by George Barna. 2002. Brentwood, TN: Integrity Publishers. P. 7).

p. 41   Peter Senge's "Creative Tension" (*The Fifth Discipline* by Peter Senge. 1990. New York: Doubleday).

p. 42   Information about the troubled Apollo 13 flight and rescue found in:(http://science.ksc.nasa.gov/history/apollo/apollo-13/apollo-13-info.html).

p. 43   Jack Welch comments: "Great organizations are all about…."
(*Winning* by Jack Welch. 2005. Harper Collins: New York)

p. 43   *Lone Survivor* by Marcus Luttrell. 2007. New York: Little, Brown & Company.

p. 44   Longfellow's belief that "All your strength is in your union…"
(http://www.bartleby.com/100/437.html)

p. 44   *Long Walk to Freedom* by Nelson Mandela. 1994. New York: Little, Brown & Company.

p. 45   Core Values of major companies: (Building Your Company's Vision *Harvard Business Review*. James C. Collins and Jerry I. Porras -- September-October 1996

p. 46   Signers of the Declaration of Independence: "Our Lives, Our Fortunes, and our Sacred Honor."
https://www.americanheritage.com

p. 46   At the entrance to West Point's football stadium is a plaque – as observed by Jim Kunau during visit to stadium.


**Chapter 5: Champions Focus on Attitude and Effort**


p. 48   "The greatest discovery of my generation…." By William James (https://www.brainyquote.com)

p. 48    Enthusiasm – Greek "En theos" – meaning rooted in God.
         (http://www.amnh.org/common/faq/quotes.html)

p. 48    Viktor Frankl - (*Man's Search for Meaning* by Viktor Frankl.
         1984.   New York: Simon & Schuster).

p. 48    Stanford Study demonstrated that 92%….. bencalfrobe.tripod.com

p. 49    Condoleeza Rice – "that she might not be able to have a hamburger
         at Woolworth's but…" (*African-American Biographies* by
         Condoleeza Rice. 2006. Illinois: Raintree.)

p. 49    Thomas Jefferson: "A person with a good attitude can
         accomplish anything." (*101 Best Ways to Land a Job in Troubled
         Times* by Jay A. Block. 2010. McGraw-Hill. P. 17).

p. 49    Zig Ziglar - … "liked to start off each day by reading both the
         newspaper and the Bible…" (*The Dallas Morning News*. By
         Robert Wilonsky. November 28, 2012)

p. 50    Margaret Thatcher: "I usually make up my mind about a man
         …."
         (*Margaret Thatcher: A Portrait of the Iron Lady* by John
         Blundell.
         2008. Algora Publishing. P.181).

p. 50    Andrew Carnegie: "… to find an ounce of gold, you have to
         mine    a ton of dirt."
         (http://www.dailyintheword.org/content/reviving-        vision)

p. 50    Mike Krzyzewski: "Before you ever utter a word, the team sees
         your face…" (*Leading With the Heart* by Mike Krzyzewski.
         2000.   New York: Business Plus).

p. 51    Vincent Peale: "…continually practice filling our minds with
         thoughts of …" (motivatedonline.com)

p. 51    (*Success is a Choice* by Rick Pitino. 1997. New York: Broadway
         Books). (Selected sentences taken from this book).

p. 51    John Wooden: "Nothing works unless you do."
          (www.wisdomquotes.com)

p. 51    Story of Pope John XXIII – https://www.nydailynews.com

p. 52    Muhammad Ali: "Suffer now and live the rest of your life as a
         Champion." (http://thinkexist.com/quotes/muhammad_ali/)

p. 52    James Froude: "You cannot dream your way into character…."
         (http://www.quotes-and-poems.com/character-quotes.html).

**Chapter 6: Champions are Motivated**


p. 54    "Live as if you were to die tomorrow..." Mahatma Gandhi – (https://www.brainyquote.com)

p. 54    John Wooden: "Make each day a masterpiece." (http://www.goodreads.com/author/quotes/23041.John_Wooden)

p. 55    Story of Joni Erickson summarized from the following: (*Joni: An Unforgettable Story* by Joni Eareckson Tada. 1976. Michigan: Zondervan).

p. 55    Albert Schweitzer: "Example is not the main thing..." (http://thinkexist.com/quotation/example_is_not_the_main_thing _in_influencing/165666.html.

p. 55    Ben Hooper story (http://stanadams.blogspot.com/2008/10/who-your-daddy-ben-hooper-story.html).

p. 57    Mike Krzyzewski: "Am I tough on the team? Absolutely. If they don't ...." (*Leading With the Heart* by Mike Krzyzewski. 2000. New York: Business Plus).

p. 58    Zig Ziglar: "97% of the people in our society do not have an organized goals program" (*Over the Top* by Zig Ziglar. 1997. Tennessee: Thomas Nelson).

p. 58    Rick Pitino – "Dreams are where we want to end up...." (*Success is a Choice* by Rick Pitino. 1997. Broadway Books: New York)

p. 58    John Wooden – "Instruction works best if it focuses learners on setting...." (*You Haven't Taught Until They Have Learned* by. Swen Nater & Ron Galimore. 2010. Virginia: Fitness Info Tech).

p. 58    Bill Snyder: "I have never said our goals..." (*Bill Snyder: They Said It Couldn't Be Done.* by Mark Janssen. 2006. KCI Sports: Champaign, IL. P. 78)

p. 59    Lou Little story - (*Called to Coach* by Bobby Bowden and Mark Schlabach. 2010. Howard Books: New York. P. 169)

p. 60    John 15:13-(The Holy Bible, New International Version. 1984. International Bible Society)

p. 60    Bill Curry: "You can't motivate someone unless you care..." (Notes acquired at the 2012 American Football Coaches Convention

p. 62    J.C. Hunter: "I have learned that employees have a subconscious..." (*The World's Most Powerful Leadership Principle* by James Hunter. 2004. Crown Business: New York)

p. 63    Statistics regarding graduation rates from high school obtained from various research articles such as the one found at: (http://www.all4ed.org/files/GraduationRates_FactSheet.pdf).

p. 63    William Glasser: "There is not enough immediate payoff either in or out of school." (*Choice Theory in the Classroom* by William Glasser. 1986. New York: Harper Collins. P. 12).

p. 63    Information on Toyota factories acquired from reading: (*How Toyota Became Number One* by David Magee. 2007. New York: Penguin Group.)

p. 64    (*You Haven't Taught Until They Have Learned* by. Swen Nater & Ron Galimore. 2010. Virginia: Fitness Info Tech).

p. 64    Wooden: "No matter how clever I designed my lesson, or how smoothly …" (*You Haven't Taught Until They Have Learned* by. Swen Nater & Ron Galimore. 2010. Virginia: Fitness Info Tech).

## Chapter 7: Champions Are Courageous

p. 66    "Courage is not the absence of fear…." Ambrose Redmoon – (https://sophia.smith.edu)

p. 66    Winston Churchill: "Courage is the most important of all virtues…" (*Plato and the Virtue of Courage* by Linda Rabieh. 2006. Maryland: John's Hopkins University Press. P. 3).

p. 67    President Reagan – "We are the land of the free …" (Speech given to Temple Hillel and Community Leaders in Valley Stream on October 26, 1984)

p. 67    Insights on Todd Beamer acquired from reading: (*Let's Roll* by Lisa Beamer. 2002. Colorado: Alive Communications).

p. 67    Gordon Brown, (*Courage: Portraits of Bravery in the Service of Great Causes*. 2008. Weinstein Books).

p. 68    John Maxwell: "His courage came from His sufficiency in His Father…" (*The Maxwell Bible* by John Maxwell. 2014. Book of John Commentaries: John 2: 13-21)

p. 68    Story of Doubting Thomas and Jesus can be found in John 20: 24-31.

p. 68    Story of Lazarus and Jesus can be found in John 11:1-44. (The Holy Bible, New International Version. 1984. International Bible Society)

p. 67    John 11:16 (The Holy Bible, New International Version. 1984. International Bible Society)

p. 69   Martin Luther King, Jr.: "With my cup of coffee sitting untouched before me…" (*Courage: Portraits of Bravery in the Service of Great Causes*. 2008. Weinstein Books).

p. 69   John Eldridge: "A man must have a fight, a great mission…" (*Wild at Heart: Discovering the Secret of Man's Soul* by John Eldridge. 2001. Tennessee: Thomas Nelson Publishing. P. 141).

p. 70   Matthew 10:28 (The Holy Bible, New International Version. 1984. International Bible Society)

p. 71   John Quincy Adams quote taken from Movie *Amistad* (1997 produced by Debbie Allen)

p. 72   Ephesians 6:12 (The Holy Bible, New International Version. 1984. International Bible Society)

p. 72   Abraham Lincoln: "The war will not be won by strategy alone…." (*Lincoln on Leadership: Executive Strategies for Tough Times* by Donald T. Phillips. 1992. New York: Warner Books).

p. 72   Information on President Mandela summarized from reading: (*Invictus* by John Carlin. 2009. USA: Penguin Publishing).

p. 73   Robert Browning: "A man's reach should exceed his grasp…" (Quote taken from Browning's poem titled: *Andrea del Sarto*. 1855.found at: http://www.sparknotes.com/poetry/browning/section10.rhtml)

p. 73   Andrew Jackson: "One man with courage makes a majority." (http://thinkexist.com/quotation/one_man_with_courage_makes_a_majority/146977.html).

p. 73   "An army of deer led by a lion is more potent than an army…" (Quote said by Phillip of Macedonia the father of Alexander the Great: http://www.youdontneedatitle.com/wordpress/?p=18).

p. 73   (*Braveheart* directed by Mel Gibson. 1995. Paramount Pictures).

p. 73   Colonel Joshua Lawrence Chamberlain's heroic efforts summarized from information acquired from the following: (*The Killer Angels* by Michael Shaara. 1987. New York: Ballantine Books). (*Gettysburg* directed by Ronald F. Maxwell. 1993. Produced by Moctesuma Esparza & Robert Katz).

p. 74   *Gladiator* (2000) Directed by Ridley Scott

p. 74   John Eldridge – "Maximus' answer builds like a wave…." (*Wild at Heart* by John Eldridge. 2001/ Thomas Nelson: Tennessee)

p. 75   Alesdandr Solzhenitzyn: "One word of truth outweighs the whole world."

(http://nobelprize.org/nobel_prizes/literature/laureates/1970/solzh
enitsyn-lecture.html)

p. 75    Miguel de Cervantes: "He who loses wealth, loses much. He who
loses …." (http://en.proverbia.net/citasautor.asp?autor=11412).


**Chapter 8: Champions are Determined**


p. 78    "Never give in…." Winston Churchill –
https://www.nationalchurchillmuseum.org

p. 78    List of defeats and failures experienced by Abraham Lincoln:
(http://sidsavara.com/personal-development/famous-failures
michael-jordan-abraham-lincoln and-jk-rowling).

p. 79    Theodore Roosevelt: "The credit belongs to the man who is
actually in the arena…" (Excerpt from a speech titled: "Citizenship in
a Republic" delivered at the Sorbonne in France on April 23,
1910:
http://sidsavara.com/personal-development/famous-failures-
michael-jordan-abraham-lincoln-and-jk-rowling).

p. 79    Geoff Colvin: "The factor that seems to explain the most about
great performance…." (*Talent is Overrated: What Really
Separates World-Class Performers from Everybody Else* by
Geoff  Colvin. 2008. New York: Penguin Group).

p. 79    Michael Phelps reported swimming for 365 days a year for five
straight years before Beijing…
(Notes acquired from hearing Michael Phelps speak at a *Get
Motivated Conference* in Anaheim, California on February 16,
2010).

p. 81    Charles Lindbergh flew 3,600 miles in 33 ½ hours in 1927…
(http://www.factmonster.com/ipka/A0004537.html).

p. 81    Lou Gehrig suffered 17 different fractured bones….
(http://www.findagrave.com/cgi-
bin/fg.cgi?page=gr&GRid=385).

p. 81    Ben Hogan was nearly killed in car accident…
(http://www.golf.com/golf/tours_news/article/0,28136,1852010,0
0.html).

p. 81    Ray Croc suffered from diabetes and had gall bladder and thyroid
gland removed….
(http://www.planetmotivation.com/ray-kroc.html).

p. 81    Apollo 1 tragedy on January 27, 1967…

(http://history.nasa.gov/apollo.html)

p. 81    John Wooden led the Bruins for 15 seasons before winning his first NCAA championship…
(http://www.uclabruins.com/sports/m-baskbl/spec-rel/ucla-wooden-page.html).

p. 81    Michael Jordan cut as a sophomore from his basketball team…
(http://www.nba.com/history/players/jordan_bio.html)

p. 81    Bethany Hamilton showed great resolve to surf following shark attack… (http://bethanyhamilton.com/about/bio/).

p. 82    Ronald Reagan: story of little boy and pony…
(http://gregghake.com/2010/02/the-pony-in-the-dung-heap-ronald-reagan-eleanor-roosevelt-and-you/).

p. 82    Sir Ernest Shackleton: "In trouble, danger, and disappointment…" (*Shackleton's Way* by Margot Morrell, Stephanie Capparell. 2001. Viking Adult: New York)

p. 83    Jim Collins: Stockdale Paradox (*Good to Great* by Jim Collins. 2001. New York: Harper Collins Publishers Inc.).

p. 84    Chip Kelly: "Win the Day. Win the drill" (SJ Magazine by Dave Spadaro)

p. 84    Matthew 6:34 (The Holy Bible, New International Version. 1984. International Bible Society)

p. 85    Chinese Farmer Story taken from a devotion book by Robert Schuller, Crystal Cathedral, Garden Grove, CA

p. 85    Roman 8:28 (The Holy Bible, New International Version. 1984. International Bible Society)

p. 85    Edward R. Murrow: "Difficulty is the excuse history never accepts."(http://www.yallagamescafe.com/quotes/edward_r_murrow/difficulty_is_the_excuse_hisory_never_accepts/).

p. 86    Chris Gardner portrayed in the movie: (*The Pursuit of Happyness* directed by Gabriele Muccino. 2006. Columbia Pictures Corporation).

p. 87    Ben Franklin – "…Never knew a man good at making excuses…." (www.wow4u.com)

p. 87    Job 1:8 (The Holy Bible, New International Version. 1984. International Bible Society)

p. 87    Corrie ten Boom – "Hold everything in your hands lightly…" (www.goodreads.com)

p. 87    Job 1:21-22 (The Holy Bible, New International Version. 1984. International Bible Society)

p. 88    Joni Erickson information acquired from: *Joni* by Joni Eareckson. 1976. Zondervan: Grand Rapids, MI

p. 88    Jim Abbott information acquired from: (http://www.jimabbott.info/biography.html).

p. 88    Tom Dempsey information acquired from: (http://www.shortbiographies.com/biographies/TomDempsey.html).

p. 88    James 1:2-3 (The Holy Bible, New International Version. 1984. International Bible Society)

p. 89    Randy Pausch: "The brick walls are not there to keep us out…." (*The Last Lecture* by Randy Pausch. 2008. New York: Hyperion).


## Chapter 9: Champions Can Communicate

p. 91    "Communication works for those who work at it." - John Powell (https://institutesuccess.com)

p. 91    Thomas Friedman's thesis synthesized from reading his book: (*The World is Flat* by Thomas Friedman. 2005. New York: Picador/Farrar, Straus & Giroux).

p. 91    George Bernard Shaw – "The single biggest problem in communication…." (www.mobile.brainyquote.com)

p. 91    Patricia Buhler: "First, people tend to assume that they know…" (*Managing in the new millennium: Six tips to more effective communication* by Patricia M. Buhler. Supervision. Wednesday, July 1, 2009: http://www.allbusiness.com/labor-employment/labor-sector-performance/12627030-1.html).

p. 92    Robert Half: "Purdue's engineering graduates were as well educated…" (*Successfully Managing Your Career Requires Good Communication*" by Robert Half. Journal of Accountancy,   00218448, Dec. 95, Vol. 180, Issue 6).

p. 92    Fredric H. Jones: "Good classroom management for teachers…." (Information acquired from attending a Fredric Jones Classroom Management Seminar in Orange, California in 1994).

p. 93    Dr. Tom Osborne: American Football Coaches Association Convention in Anaheim, California (1994).

p. 94    Professor Ellen Fitzpatrick: "… became freighted with deeper meaning."(http://www.usnews.com/news/politics/articles/2008/01/17/a-damaging-impatience).

p. 94	Indira Gandhi: "You cannot shake hands with a clenched fist."
	(http://www.quotationspage.com/quote/1117.html).

p. 95	St. Francis: "Preach the Gospel at all times…"
	(http://thinkexist.com/quotation/preach_the_gospel_at_all_times
	_and_when_necessary/219332.html).

p. 95	Mark Twain: "There are two types of speakers…."
	(http://www.presentation-
	pointers.com/showarticle/articleid/187/).

p. 95	Story of President Lincoln's response to Dr. Finnes Gurley's
	sermon…(http://www.greatleadershipbydan.com/2011/02/3-
	simple-presentation-tips-for-leaders.html).

p. 96	President Kennedy's famous quotes.
	(http://www.quotationspage.com/quotes/John_F._Kennedyhttp://
	www.quotationspage.com/quotes/John_F._Kennedy)
	(http://history1900s.about.com/od/1960s/a/jfkmoon.htm)

p. 97	(*The Lost Art of Listening* by Michael Nichols. 1995. New York:
	Guilford Press).

**Chapter 10: Champions Create a Culture of Unity**

p. 100	"Alone we can do so little…." - Helen Keller –
	(https://www.brainyquote.com)

p. 101	Psalm 133:1 (The Holy Bible, New International Version. 1984.
	International Bible Society)

p. 101	Colonel Hal Moore: W.E. stood for *Without Equal*
	(*We Were Soldiers* directed by Randall Wallace. 2002. Paramount
	Pictures).

p. 101	Pat Riley: "The disease of Me leads to the defeat of Us."
	(*The Winner Within* by Pat Riley. 1993. New York: Berkley
	Books).

p. 101	Benjamin Franklin: "We must, indeed, all hang together….."
	https://www.brainyquote.com

p. 101	Pastor Andy Stanley–"Whoever devotes themselves to themselves…."
	(www.resolutionseries.org)

p. 102	Nelson Mandela: (*Long Walk to Freedom* by Nelson Mandela.
	1995. Little Brown @ Co.: Boston, MA

p. 103	Vince Lombardi: "Build for your team a feeling…"
	https://quotefancy.com

	p. 104	Martin Luther King: "Everyone can be great because

everyone can serve."
(http://thinkexist.com/quotation/everyone_can_be_great_
because_everyone_can/346363.html).

p. 104  Matthew 20:26 (The Holy Bible, New International Version.
1984. International Bible Society)

## Chapter 11: Champions Strive to Rise Above Doom

p. 106  "It takes 20 years to build a reputation…." - Warren Buffett) –
(https://www.cnbc.com)

p. 106  Genesis 3:17 (The Holy Bible, New International Version. 1984.
International Bible Society)

p. 107  John 3:16 (The Holy Bible, New International Version. 1984.
International Bible Society)

p. 107  President Harry Truman: "Power, money, and women."
(*Truman* by David McCullough. 1992. New York: Simon &
Schuster).

p. 107  1 Samuel 10:24 (The Holy Bible, New International Version.
1984. International Bible Society)

p. 108  2 Samuel 11:2-3 (The Holy Bible, New International Version.
1984. International Bible Society)

p. 108  James Dobson: "25% of the daily internet searches …."
(As communicated on a radio broadcast and supported by Rachel
Alexander at www.mobile.wind.com)

p. 109  Genesis 4:8 (The Holy Bible, New International Version. 1984.
International Bible Society)

p. 109  Ephesians 4:26 (The Holy Bible, New International Version.
1984. International Bible Society)

p. 109  Exodus 2:11-14 (The Holy Bible, New International Version.
1984. International Bible Society)

p. 110  Exodus 32:15-20 (The Holy Bible, New International Version.
1984. International Bible Society)

p. 110  Exodus 34:1 (The Holy Bible, New International Version. 1984.
International Bible Society)

p. 110  Numbers 12:3 (The Holy Bible, New International Version.
1984. International Bible Society)

p. 111  Numbers 20:8-12 (The Holy Bible, New International Version.
1984. International Bible Society)

p. 111  General George Patton: "While visiting wounded soldiers in the

army hospital…"
(http://www.scribd.com/doc/35629722/Anger-Allen-M-Baker).

p. 112 Woody Hayes litany of anger issues taken from the following site: (http://www.time.com/time/magazine/article/0,9171,920009,00.html).

p. 112 James 1:19-20 (The Holy Bible, New International Version. 1984. International Bible Society)

p. 112 Romans 7:18-19 (The Holy Bible, New International Version. 1984. International Bible Society)

## Chapter 12: Champions Influence Others

p. 115 "There is no power on earth that can…."- Booker T. Washington- (https://www.brainyquote.com)

p. 116 John Maxwell: "Leadership is Influence."
(*The 21 Irrefutable Laws of Leadership* by John Maxwell. 1998. Nashville: Thomas Nelson Publishers).

p. 117 (*Raving Fans* by Ken Blanchard. 1993. New York: William Morrow Company, Inc.).

p. 118 Eleanor Roosevelt – "You can never really live anyone else's ….. (www.mobil.brainyquote.com)

p. 119 Story of Jim Joyce synthesized from information acquired from: (http://www.aolnews.com/2010/06/02/umpire-jim-joyces-blown-call-costs-armando-galaragga-perfect-ga/).

p. 119 Credibility: Latin word credo which means "I believe." (http://dictionary.reference.com/browse/credible).

p. 120 Dan Cathy – "Leaders must first take care of their employees…" (Information learned at a seminar conducted by Dan Cathy on the campus of Concordia University Irvine.)

p. 120 James' Hunters book: (*The Servant* by James Hunter. 1998. The Doubleday Religious Publishing Group: New York)

# About the Authors

Jim Kunau is an accomplished coach, educator, and leader. During his 19 seasons as the Head Football Coach at Orange Lutheran High School, Jim relentlessly pursued the mission of his football program: *Building Champions for Life*. In the process his teams won 13 league titles as well as two sectional and one state championship. His teams were ranked as high as #8 in the nation, and he was inducted into the Orange Lutheran Hall of Fame in 2017. In his five seasons at Rancho Christian High School he won another sectional and state championship, making him one of only two coaches in California history to win state titles at more than one school. Jim has also served as Athletic Director, Executive Director, high school teacher and college instructor. Since 2012, he has taught leadership classes in, and now serves as Director of Concordia University Irvine's renowned Masters in Coaching and Athletic Administration program, helping to develop transformational coaches and leaders in athletics.

Among his honors are being selected the Orange County (CA) Coach of the Decade, Nike National Coach of the Year, Cal Hi Sports California Coach of the Year, Los Angeles Times Southern California Coach of the Year. He has spoken on organizational leadership all over the United States.

Jim resides in Anaheim Hills, California with his wife Betsy and daughter Caroline.

# About the Authors

Kent Schlichtemeier loves to teach! He began his career in 1978 teaching 6th-8th grades in Oxnard, CA. After completing his Master's degree at the University of Denver in 1984, he taught at the high school level in Orlando, FL. Kent served as a Professor in the School of Education at Concordia University Irvine from 1988-2003 where he mentored future teachers. In addition to teaching at Concordia, Kent was the women's basketball coach until retiring from coaching in 1993 to pursue his doctorate degree. During the final two seasons of Kent's tenure as coach, the Lady Eagle Basketball team made two consecutive appearances at the NAIA National Basketball Tournament after winning the Golden State Athletic Conference Championships. Kent was named the District Three NAIA Coach of the Year in 1992 and 1993 and was inducted into the Concordia Athletic Hall of Fame in 2006.

In 1996, Kent completed his Ed.D. at UCLA in Educational Leadership. Kent served as a teacher and Assistant Principal at Orange Lutheran High School from 2003-2007 before returning to teach at Concordia University Irvine. Today, Kent serves as the Dean of the School of Education. Kent enjoys frequent opportunities to speak at sports banquets, school graduations, teacher conferences, leadership retreats, and business seminars. Kent and his wife Cindy, son Aaron, and daughter Kayla live in Irvine.